10000 Mk.
Wer ist
Seit Montag, dem 11. Juni ds.
Der Schüler Kurt Klawitzky und
gewesen Müllerstr.
Aus verschiedenen
ähnlichen
Jahres

CLASSIC
FILM
SCRIPTS

M

a film by

Fritz Lang

English translation and description of action
by Nicholas Garnham

Simon and Schuster, New York

ACKNOWLEDGEMENTS

We wish to thank Nicola Croke and Martin Hayden for their assistance in this book. Our thanks are also due to Nero Films International, L'Avant Scène du Cinéma and the British Film Institute for the use of their stills.

INTRODUCTION

Perhaps the key sequence in *M* is the one in which Lang cuts back and forth between a meeting of underworld leaders and a meeting of police chiefs. He uses every means at his command to equate these two groups, inter-cutting, camera angles and groupings, the same smoke-filled light, overlapping gestures and speech. This equation of what are traditionally seen in gangster pictures as good and evil, is central to Lang's universe. The world he portrays is a Manichean one in which the forces of good and evil, equally matched, constantly fight for man's soul as the police and the underworld both relentlessly pursue M the murderer.

Lang's favourite image for this dualism is the mirror. For it is significant that the murderer first sees the M on his back, the mark of Cain, in a mirror. M also is a letter whose mirror-image is the same as its real self.

This mirroring is carried right through the structure of the film. For the conflict between good and evil within the murderer himself, the *doppel-gänger* who haunts him, is itself a reflection of the conflict between crime and the law.

At this period Lang took a view of the law similar to Aeschylus. It is a symbol of God's order on earth. It is the one bulwark against chaos and therefore at the end of *M* it is presented as a saviour.

It is this closeness to classical Greek morality that Godard explored when he got Lang to play himself in *Le Mépris,* a film in which the German director is making a film of *The Odyssey.* In Lang's work we see the director looking down on his world like some Greek god, imposing a pattern on the warring universe. Lang himself has said that his constant concern has been man fighting his destiny. And this destiny is represented by Lang's style, by the very mechanics of film-making. His awareness of the forces of evil and chaos, always on the prowl, makes him fasten like a vice round his world and his characters. Unlike directors such as Renoir or Mitzoguchi, Lang can never allow his characters or his audience to feel free. Every shot has a specific structure in which his characters are trapped as in a spider's web. The camera is constantly looking down, imposing itself on the characters. And Lang's editing style locks every shot to the preceding and succeeding shot in sequences that drag the characters remorselessly forward like some inescapable fate. In Lang, editing is functional. When a character makes a suggestion or has a thought, as often as not the next shot illustrates the results of that suggestion or thought. So man is always being brought to face the results of his conduct.

It is in this sense that Lang is such a remorseless moralist, and such a pure film-maker. Unlike Renoir, for instance, neither accident nor mercy really enters his world. Everything is governed by an inexorable logic. In Lang's last film, *The 1,000 Eyes of Dr. Mabuse,* the whole world has been reduced to a vast hotel over which his evil genius watches by means of television cameras. A director in a television control room, dictating a pattern of action by selection from his all-seeing eyes, is Lang's vision of God.

At the time of *M,* Lang's vision was still optimistic. He believed that order could overcome chaos, but under the impact first of Hitler and then of American society, this optimism crumbled. In *Fury,* the law court has become an obscene joke. In *You Only Live Once,* the forces of law and order are seen as remorseless, impersonal forces destroying personal happiness. In *The Big Heat,* the hero has to leave the police force and take on the characteristics of a gangster in order to revenge himself on his wife's killers.

Yet the mirror-image and the fight between good and evil persists. In *You Only Live Once,* the happy honeymooners are seen reflected in a pool during their brief moment of happiness; a stone disturbs the water and they are on their way to inevitable death.

In *Woman in the Window,* Edward G. Robinson, a quiet respectable business-man, has a terrible nightmare in which he is involved in adultery and murder. The nightmare and the reality are presented in an identically similar style. One is a mirror image of the other and it shows vividly how thin

10

and fragile is the barrier that protects us from our other self. In Lang's world man must be constantly on his guard against his own personal furies. The façade of ordered, rational behaviour is hardly strong enough to contain the boiling destrutive urges that we all share. Indeed, in *M*, Lang uses the ironies implicit in a trial conducted by criminals to point a finger at us all. None of you is innocent, he says. None of you is safe. Morality is a process of constant vigilance and battle.

NICHOLAS GARNHAM

CREDITS:

Produced by	Nero Film A.G.
Directed by	Fritz Lang
Scenario and dialogue by	Thea von Harbou
after an article by	Egon Jacobson
In collaboration with	Paul Falkenberg, Adolf Jansen and Karl Vash
Murderer's theme by	Edward Grieg : extract from ' Peer Gynt '
Director of photography	Fritz Arno Wagner
Camera operator	Karl Vash
Chief editor	Paul Falkenberg
Designed by	Emil Hasler and Karl Vollbrecht
Film shot during	Six weeks in 1931
Original length	Two hours
Length of actual film	1 hour 39 mins.
Process	Black and white (normal screen)

CAST:

Hans Beckert, the murderer	Peter Lorre
Inspector Lohmann	Otto Wernicke
Schränker, head of the underworld	Gustaf Gründgens
Mrs. Beckmann	Ellen Widmann
Elsie Beckmann	Inge Landgut
Chief of police	Ernst Stahl-Nachbaur
The Minister	Franz Stein
Inspector Groeber	Theodor Loos
The burglar	Fritz Gnass
The safe-breaker	Fritz Odemar
The pick-pocket	Paul Kemp
The con-man	Theo Lingen
The blind beggar	Georg John
The night watchman	Karl Platen
The Inspector's secretary	Gerhard Bienert
The landlady of the ' Crocodile Club '	Rosa Valetti
A prostitute	Hertha von Walther
The lawyer	Rudolf Blümner

with : Almas, Balhaus, Behal Carell, Dahmen, Döblin, Eckof, Else Ehser, Elzer, Faber, Ilse Fürstenberg, Gelingk, Goldstein, Goltz, Heinrich Gotho, Gretler, Hadank, Hartberg, Hempel, Hocker, Hoermann, Isenta, Karchow, Kepich, Hermann Krehan, Kurth Leeser, Rose Lichtenstein, Lotte Löbinger, Lohde, Loretto, Maschek, Matthis, Méderow, Margarete Melzer, Trude Moos, Netto, Neumann, Nied, Maja Norden, Edgar Pauly, Klaus Pohl, Polland, Rebane, Paul Rehkopf, Reihsig, Rhaden, Ritter, Sablotzky, Sascha, Agnes Schulz-Lichterfeld, Leonhard Steckel, Stroux, Swinborne, Trutz, Otto Waldis, Walth, Wanka, Wannemann, Wulf, Ziener and members of the underworld, police or people of the town

M

Close-up of a large white M on a black screen. At the end, over the black screen, the titles unroll and a child's voice is heard singing.

Shot from above of a group of children standing in a circle, playing a game. In the centre of the circle a little girl passes from one to another, chanting.

LITTLE GIRL : Just you wait a little while,

The evil man in black will come.

With his little chopper,

He will chop you up.

The LITTLE GIRL *stops in front of one of her playmates and gestures to her to leave the circle.*

LITTLE GIRL : You're out.

The child leaves the circle and the game continues.

LITTLE GIRL : Just you wait a little while,

The evil man in black will come.

With his little chopper,

He will chop you up.

During the song, the camera pans off to show two coal-bunkers in the courtyard of a block of flats. The camera climbs the face of the tenement block to show an outside balcony with washing hanging out to dry. A pregnant woman appears, carrying a basket of laundry; she leans over the balcony and shouts down to the children.

WOMAN : Will you stop singing that awful song . . . *The singing continues off* . . . Can't you hear? . . . *Mutters to herself* . . . Always that awful song.

She disappears and the song continues.

LITTLE GIRL : Just you wait a little while,

The evil man in black will come.

With his little chopper . . .

Cut to the narrow staircase of the tenement block. Shot from above, we see the front door of one of the flats. In front of the door, the WOMAN *with the basket of laundry rings the bell. The camera tracks in as the door opens and a tired, haggard, middle-aged woman appears. It is* MRS. BECKMANN. *Behind her, we see a kitchen. The* WOMAN *hands the basket to* MRS. BECKMANN *and wearily wipes her brow. During the following dialogue, a rapid series of cuts takes place between the two women.*

WOMAN *sighing:* Oh, dear!

MRS. BECKMANN: What's the matter?

WOMAN: I'm always telling those kids to stop singing that terrible murderer's song . . . and they do nothing but sing it at the top of their voices all day . . . *A pause.* As if we hadn't heard enough of that murderer.

MRS. BECKMANN: Oh, leave them alone. As long as they're singing, at least we know they're still there.

WOMAN: Yes, I suppose you're right.

She shrugs her shoulders and shuffles away.

Camera pans with MRS. BECKMANN, *as she shuts the door and puts the basket of washing in a corner of the kitchen. Pan with her to reveal a poor but clean kitchen.* MRS. BECKMANN *bends over a bowl of water and continues with her washing. Medium close-up of her. A cuckoo-clock strikes. As* MRS. BECKMANN *looks up, the camera follows her eyes to a close-up of the cuckoo-clock, which shows midday. The ringing of a church bell mingles with the cuckoos. Cut back to* MRS. BECKMANN, *who straightens up, drying her hands.*

In the street, a group of parents is waiting on the pavement outside the main entrance to the local school. Cars pass. The bell stops ringing as the children come out; one little girl waves and goes off in a different direction to her friends. It is ELSIE BECKMANN; *she has a satchel on her back and carries a string bag with a ball in it. When she comes to cross the road she steps off the kerb without looking, a car hoots at her and she steps back onto the kerb. A policeman stops the traffic and escorts her across. In the kitchen,* MRS. BECKMANN *is laying the table. In the street,* ELSIE *runs along the pavement of a busy road, bouncing her ball. She stops by a circular pillar of the sort used as a billboard and starts throwing her ball*

16

against it. The camera follows the ball and tracks in to show one of the posters.

10,000 Marks Reward
WHO IS THE MURDERER?
Since Monday, 11th June this year, the following have disappeared: the school-children KLAUS KLAWITZKY *and his sister* KLARA, *who live at 470 Müller Street. Various evidence leads us to believe that the children were victims of a similar crime to that committed last autumn against the* DOERING *sisters.*

As the ball continues to bounce against the poster, the shadow of a man in a hat falls across the pillar: it is the shadow of the murderer. (Still on page 1)
MURDERER *off* : What a pretty ball. *The shadow bends down.* What's your name?
ELSIE *off* : Elsie Beckmann.
In the kitchen, MRS BECKMANN *is peeling potatoes and putting them into a tureen. Quick cut to the clock. It is 12.20. Cut back to* MRS. BECKMANN, *who puts the lid on the tureen. She hears footsteps, goes to the door, opens it and looks up the stairs. Two little girls are going up.*
MRS. BECKMANN : Elsie didn't come with you?
1ST LITTLE GIRL : No.
2ND LITTLE GIRL *simultaneously* : No, she didn't come with us.
Cut back to MRS. BECKMANN *who watches from the doorway, as the girls go on up the stairs; then she leans over the bannisters. The camera tilts straight down the empty staircase well. Cut back to* MRS. BECKMANN *who goes back into her flat.*
Shot from high above, as a beggar is seen walking along the pavement of a busy street. Camera tracks in slightly to show the card hung round the beggar's neck, which reads BLIND. He stops at a corner to sell balloons. A paper windmill is stuck in his battered hat. The MURDERER *and* ELSIE *stand beside him examining the balloons. The* MURDERER *whistles, loudly and off-key, the*

first bars of a tune from Grieg's ' Peer Gynt.' He buys a balloon in the shape of a huge doll and hands it to ELSIE *who thanks him with a little curtsey.*

ELSIE : Thank you very much. (*Still on page 2*)

Cut back to the kitchen, where MRS. BECKMANN *is putting the tureen into a steaming saucepan. The bell rings. Pan with her, as she rushes to open the door. On the doorstep stands the* PAPERMAN.

PAPERMAN : Good morning . . . A thrilling new chapter, Mrs. Beckmann! *He hands her the paper.* Passionate, moving, sensational . . .

MRS. BECKMANN *very wearily* : Good — thank you. *A pause.* Oh . . . just a moment, Mr. Gehrke.

She takes the paper and moves away. Camera stays on the PAPERMAN.

MRS. BECKMAN *off* : Tell me, Mr. Gehrke . . .

PAPERMAN : Yes?

MRS. BECKMAN *off* : Have you seen Elsie?

PAPERMAN : Didn't she just come up the stairs?

MRS. BECKMANN *comes back to the door to pay the* PAPERMAN. *Shot of the two of them.*

MRS. BECKMANN : No, she's not back yet.

PAPERMAN : Well, she won't be long now. *He touches the peak of his cap and turns to go.* Good-bye, Mrs. Beckmann.

MRS. BECKMANN : Good-bye, Mr. Gehrke.

She hesitates for a moment, then goes onto the landing and leans once again over the bannisters. The camera tilts straight down the empty staircase well.

MRS. BECKMANN *off, her voice echoing* : Elsie! Elsie!

Cut back to MRS. BECKMANN *who, looking worried, goes back to her flat and closes the door. Camera follows. Close-up of the cuckoo-clock which shows 1.15; the cuckoo strikes once. Long shot of the room:* MRS. BECKMANN *opens the window and leans out, calling anxiously.*

MRS. BECKMANN : Elsie! Elsie!

Cut to a tilt straight down the empty staircase well.

MRS. BECKMANN *off* : Elsie!

Cut to the loft of the block of flats, empty except for some washing hanging in the shadows.

MRS. BECKMANN *off* : Elsie!

Medium close-up, shot slightly from above, of Elsie's empty chair at the kitchen table: her clean plate, her spoon, and her folded serviette.

MRS. BECKMANN *still calling off* : Elsie! Elsie!

Medium close-up of a patch of scrubby ground. Out of the undergrowth, rolls ELSIE'S *ball. It stops in the middle of frame. The big, doll-shaped balloon, floats up and catches momentarily in some telegraph wires, until the wind shakes it free and carries it away.*

MRS. BECKMANN *off* : Elsie!

Fade to black.

High shot from above of a street. Close-up of a car parked at the kerb. A PAPERSELLER *rushes by waving the latest edition.*

PAPERSELLER : Extra! Extra! Extra!

A passer-by stops him and buys a paper.

High shot from above of a different street. A PAPER-SELLER *can be seen, surrounded by a crowd.*

PAPERSELLER : Extra! Extra! New crime! Who is the murderer? Who! Who is the murderer?

Inside his room, the MURDERER *is seated at the window-sill, his back to the camera, writing. He has a cigarette in his left hand and is still whistling the tune from ' Peer Gynt.' Through the double windows, can be seen some fruit and other food. The camera tilts down on him and tracks in until we can see what he is writing. The hand-writing is childish.*

' Since the police haven't published my first letter, I am writing today straight to the NEWSPAPERS. Keep up your investigations. Everything will happen just as I have predicted. But I haven't yet FINISHED.'

Close-up of a police poster. We have time to read:

10,000 Marks Reward
WHO IS THE MURDERER?

Then the camera tracks back to show a crowd gathered round the poster. General hubbub.

VOICES OF CROWD : Good God, off we go again . . . It's

terrible! . . . 10,000 Marks . . . The lettering is too small, we can't read it all! . . . Hey, read it out loud, you, there in front . . . Yes, read it . . . out loud . . . *Reading* ' The un-known murderer ' . . . Let him read. Oh, hey! . . . Quiet! . . . Shut up! . . . *Reading* ' The terror in our town has found a new ' . . . Oh, that's enough . . . Stop it! . . . *reading* ' victim ' . . . Louder, we can't hear a thing.

> *The sound of the crowd mixes to the voice of a* RADIO ANNOUNCER.

RADIO ANNOUNCER : Certain evidence leads us to believe that the murderer is the same as the one who has already killed eight children in our town. We must once more draw your attention to the fact.

> *Shot from above, we see a group of middle-class men sitting round a café table, smoking and drinking. One of them, an* OLD MAN, *reads aloud from a newspaper. His voice takes over from the* RADIO ANNOUNCER. *In the middle of the table, stands a little embroidered flag, the insignia of the club to which these gentlemen belong.*

OLD MAN *reading* : ' That the first duty of every mother, of every father, is to warn their children of the danger which always threatens them. Moreover, because the danger is often hidden under an attractive disguise : some sweets, a toy, fruit, can be the murderer's weapons.'

THE OTHER MEN : Very true. Of course.

> *The* OLD MAN *stops reading to take a gulp of beer. His neighbour, a fat civil servant in a stiff collar, impati-ently stuffs a huge cigar into a cigar-holder.*

MAN WITH CIGAR HOLDER : Go on . . . *Nervously* . . . Come on now, read on.

OLD MAN : Right, right . . . *reading* . . . ' The anxiety of the general public is all the greater, because police enquiries . . .'

> *Cut to two of the other men at the table. Close-up of a bald man wearing pince-nez; beside him, a little to one side, a fat man twirls a glass of wine in his hand. Over this shot, the voice of the* OLD MAN *continues reading.*

OLD MAN *off* : '. . . have not yet finished. But the police find themselves faced by an almost impossible problem.'

> *The* BALD MAN *nudges his neighbour and they whisper*

20

to one another.

The BALD MAN *points his cigar at the man opposite him. The* OLD MAN *continues to read.*

OLD MAN *off*: 'The guilty man has left no trace. Who is the murderer?'

Cut to the man opposite listening attentively. On his cigar-holder, we see the design of a naked woman. Occasionally, the head of The OLD MAN *appears in the left of frame.*

OLD MAN *continues*: 'What is he like? Where is he hiding? No one knows. And, yet, he is one of us. Your neighbour could be the murderer.'

He lowers the paper. Cut to The BALD MAN *and his small companion who stares with contempt at the* MAN WITH CIGAR-HOLDER. *On the table, the newspaper 'Tempo', with the headline: '10,000 Marks reward'. The* BALD MAN *grabs his glass of beer.*

BALD MAN: Yes, that's right.

High shot of the whole group from above.

MAN WITH CIGAR-HOLDER: Why do you look at me, when you say that?

BALD MAN: You know very well.

MAN WITH CIGAR-HOLDER: What do I know very well?

Medium close-up of the BALD MAN *behind his glass of beer; he leans forwards and stares at his companion through his pince-nez.*

BALD MAN: All right . . . think a bit. You'll find out.

Camera cuts between them as they speak.

MAN WITH CIGAR-HOLDER: What are you insinuating?

BALD MAN: That I saw you going up the stairs, behind the little girl from the fourth floor.

MAN WITH CIGAR-HOLDER *jumps up, shouting angrily:* What? You're mad, you swine!

BALD MAN *also jumps up, shouting*: Who's a swine? Me? Me? Or the man who chases little girls?

In the excitement, he loses his pince-nez. Shot from above of the whole group.

MAN WITH CIGAR-HOLDER *mad with rage*: Bastard! Swine!

BALD MAN *in the same state*: Murderer . . . murderer!

As the MAN WITH CIGAR-HOLDER *tries to punch his opponent, two friends and a waiter intervene. There is general confusion.*

OLD MAN : But, gentlemen! . . . Gentlemen! Gentlemen!

MAN WITH CIGAR-HOLDER : You . . . me? Both of us! *They are separated.* I'll see you in court.

BALD MAN : I'll see *you* in court.

WAITER *intervening* : Now then, gentlemen . . . calm down.

ANOTHER CLIENT : I didn't mean to . . .

The HEAD WAITER, *a* CLIENT *and the three friends go out. The* SMALL MAN *has been watching the row with fiendish glee. The* BALD MAN *continues to shout at his departing enemy.*

BALD MAN : Slanderer . . . ruining my reputation.

Cut to a long shot of a bedroom in a comfortable bourgeois flat. The drawers of a chest have been pulled out and the contents scattered everywhere. Through the door we see a sitting-room.

A VOICE : What a slanderer! What an awful man!

A woman appears at the doorway, in tears.

THE VOICE *continues* : And the police listened to him! . . . They're searching my house!

A POLICEMAN *and* THE HUSBAND *come through the door into the sitting room.*

THE WOMAN *weeping* : What shame! . . . Oh, what shame!

THE HUSBAND : Searching an honest man's flat, because of an anonymous letter. It's . . . it's . . .

POLICEMAN *calmly* : Mr. Jäger, calm down. We're only doing our duty.

THE HUSBAND : When we never have a minute's peace? Frightened about the children . . .

POLICEMAN : Look here. For that very reason, the police must follow every lead . . . Any man in the street . . . *cut to a man in the street* . . . could be the guilty man.

It is evening. In the street, a little man of about sixty, wearing a bowler hat and spectacles with round, metal rims stops under a street lamp to read his paper. A LITTLE GIRL *comes up to him, pushing a scooter.*

LITTLE GIRL : Could you tell me what time it is, please?

26

OLD MAN *very friendly*: Yes, my child . . . *He takes out his watch.*

A few yards away, in front of a furniture shop, two shoppers, laden with parcels, look on. A WORKMAN *with huge wide shoulders, wearing a cap, comes out of the shop.*
Camera cuts back to the LITTLE GIRL, *who stands with her back to the camera, with the* OLD MAN *in the bowler hat facing her. In the background, the big* WORK-MAN *approaches, menacingly. The* OLD MAN *puts his watch away and bends down to the* LITTLE GIRL.

OLD MAN: Now, my child, you must go home . . . Where do you live?

As the LITTLE GIRL *goes off on her scooter, the* WORK-MAN *interrupts.*

WORKMAN: What business is it of yours, where the kid lives?

OLD MAN *looking up terrified*: Excuse me?

Medium close-up shot from above of the OLD MAN *looking up anxiously, through his pebbled-glasses, with great, round, scared eyes.*
Shot from below of the WORKMAN, *who, enormous, rises on his toes.*

WORKMAN: What did you want with the kid?

OLD MAN *startled*: But . . . but . . . nothing at all! And you, what do you want with me?

The WORKMAN *seizes his arm. Some people stop and gather round.*

WORKMAN *seizing the* OLD MAN: Just you wait and see.

OLD MAN *struggling*: Let go . . . Let me go. It's a . . . a . . . an impertinence!

FIRST PASSER-BY: What's going on?

OLD MAN *to* PASSER-BY: It's an outrage!

SECOND PASSER-BY: What does he want, the one in specs?

WORKMAN *to* OLD MAN: Don't get on your high horse.

WORKMAN *to* SECOND PASSER-BY: First, he accosts child-ren . . .

ANOTHER BYSTANDER: Punch his face in!

WORKMAN *continuing*: . . . and then, he comes on all high and mighty.

OLD MAN *struggling*: Let me go, can't you? I didn't start the conversation with the child.

WORKMAN: You wanted to get off with her, didn't you?

PASSER-BY *violently*: Yes . . . and then kill her like all the others . . . eh? *Everyone joins in and starts shouting.*

CROWD: It's the murderer! . . . It's him! . . . Hold onto him. Call the police . . . Of course, no cops when you need them . . . Oh, constable . . . constable . . .

Everyone hangs onto the OLD MAN. (Still on page 3)
Shot from above of the stairs of a double-decker bus; the crowd can be seen jostling and calling for a policeman.

CROWD: Constable . . . constable.

The CONDUCTOR comes down the stairs pushing people out of the way.

CONDUCTOR: Move along, please . . . move along now . . . stop blocking the way.

Behind the CONDUCTOR, comes a POLICEMAN, leading a THIEF.

THE THIEF *insultingly*: You're good at catching pickpockets, that's all you know how to do . . . You'd do better to go after the child murderer.

A dense crowd presses against the bus.

VARIOUS VOICES: What? The child murderer? The murderer . . . That's him . . . the murderer!

POLICEMAN: Move along now. *To the* THIEF. Come on now . . . get a move on.

Hysterical cries rise from the crowd. Fists are raised. The POLICEMAN and his prisoner have difficulty forcing their way through. Dissolve.

Close-up of the headlines of a daily paper, 'Tempo':
'THE MURDERER WRITES TO THE PAPERS'
Underneath, the MURDERER's letter is reproduced.
'Since the police haven't published my first letter, I am writing today straight to the NEWSPAPERS. Keep up your investigations. Everything will happen just as I have predicted. But I haven't yet FINISHED.'
A hand nervously holding a monocle spreads out the paper. It is the MINISTER; he sits at his deck, in his office,

the newspaper spread out before him. He is speaking into a white telephone, emphasising his points with wooden gestures.

MINISTER : It's an unheard-of scandal . . . What a deplorable effect this will have on public opinion, Inspector. It is a serious error, very serious.

Cut to the Office of the Chief of Police. The CHIEF OF POLICE, *an elegant man, is seated at his desk. In one hand, he waves a pen; in the other, he holds the telephone.*

CHIEF OF POLICE : But, Minister, we've got no power to prevent the murderer from writing to anyone he wants to !

The MINISTER'S *reply is inaudible. The* CHIEF OF POLICE *is passed some letters to sign, by his secretary. As he is leaving, the* CHIEF OF POLICE *signs to him to note a meeting in his engagement book. The* SECRETARY *does so and leaves.*

CHIEF OF POLICE *into the telephone* : The guilty man is a mental case. He must get pleasure out of seeing his actions reported in the papers. We immediately got in touch with the editor to obtain the original letter. The laboratory is already busy on it.

Large close-up of a set of finger-prints in the Police laboratory. It is the dossier of a certain Richard Ernst, known as ' Four-Fingered Ernst.' Pan across the dossier to show the prints of the left hand, next to the right.

CHIEF OF POLICE *off* : Of course, it is almost impossible to find usable finger-prints on a postcard that has been through so many hands.

Close-up of a hand moving a magnifying glass across a dossier.

CHIEF OF POLICE *off* : But we must try everything . . .

In another room in the police laboratory, a finger-print is projected onto a large screen. Silhouetted against it a police research assistant compares the projection with the dossier, with the aid of a magnifying glass.

CHIEF OF POLICE *off* : . . . to find in our archives a clue or a trail that will lead us nearer a solution.

Cut to the office of the police archives where an employee

29

is pacing up and down dictating a report.

Back in his room, the MURDERER *looks at himself in the mirror and makes terrible faces, spreading his lips and lifting his eyebrows with his fingers. (Still on page 3)*

Close-up of the MINISTER, *on the telephone in his office.*

THE MINISTER: Yes, yes, Inspector . . . certainly. I don't doubt your keenness . . . the efforts of your men . . . But, all the same . . . the result. *Annoyed.* We must have results . . . results.

The sound of The MINISTER'S *voice continues as we cut to the* CHIEF OF POLICE'S *office. He puts down the receiver which continues to crackle '*results . . . results.*' He drums his fingers nervously on his desk, then picks up the receiver. During the following conversation the* CHIEF OF POLICE'S *voice continues as images illustrate what he is saying.*

CHIEF OF POLICE: Minister, my men are only getting twelve hours' sleep a week. . . .

A police-station at night. Several tired policemen slump on benches. As two come in off their beats another two get up and go out.

CHIEF OF POLICE: . . . as well as searches on the spot, Minister.

High shot from above of suburban gardens. Plain-clothes men are seen searching everywhere. In the background are two photographers. A flash-gun goes off. Behind a hedge one of the policemen finds a ball of paper.

CHIEF OF POLICE *off*: . . . We find, for instance, behind a hedge in a thicket a little tissue-paper bag . . .

Close-up of a pair of tweezers carefully lifting the paper-bag on which can be read the word SWEETS.

CHIEF OF POLICE *off*: . . . clearly it held cheap sweets . . . In a corner we found tiny crumbs of acid drops and some grains of coloured sugar. Within a radius of twelve kilometres, we have . . .

Close-up of a map of Berlin. The gardens where the bag was discovered are circled and dated '21-6'. A compass draws a second larger circle dated '22-6'; the same compass starts a third circle.

CHIEF OF POLICE *off*: . . . searched in all the sweet-shops,

cake-shops, to find out where the bag came from . . . In vain
. . . every day we widen the area of the search . . .

*At the counter of a sweet-shop, a detective questions a
sales-girl who shakes her head.*

Chief of Police *off* : . . . but, of course, no one remembers
anything . . . or, at least not clearly enough . . .

*At a sweet and ice-cream kiosk, a detective questions a
salesman, without success.*

Chief of Police : . . . In spite of all these negative replies we
are keeping up the search, stepping more and more into an
area of uncertainty . . .

*At a grocer's, a detective questions a grocer and his wife,
without success.*

Chief of Police : . . . without much hope of finding any
solution. Our men . . .

Cut to the Minister's *office. Medium close-up of him
crashing his palm violently against his desk, his other
hand holding the telephone.*

Minister *furious* : What good is that to me? Inspector, I
know you're not sleeping . . . but those are the facts : an
unknown murderer terrorizes the town . . . a town of four
million people . . . And . . . and . . . the police, *your* police,
are failing.

Medium close-up of the Chief of Police *at his desk.
He is annoyed by what the* Minister *has just said.*

Chief of Police *irritated* : Minister, you don't really seem to
appreciate the incredible difficulties which face us.

In an office at Police HQ a Detective *questions two
witnesses. One is large and fat; he wears a little beard
and pince-nez. The other witness is stunted. In the background is a typist.*

1st Witness *indignantly to* 2nd Witness : You don't know
anything.

2nd Witness *leaping from his chair* : More than you, sir.

Detective : But, gentlemen, gentlemen . . . Could you at
least come to some agreement on what colour bonnet the
little girl was wearing, who you saw talking to an unknown
man this morning?

1st Witness : But, of course, Inspector, the bonnet was red.

31

2ND WITNESS : Inspector, the bonnet was green.

1ST WITNESS *rising* : It was a red bonnet.

2ND WITNESS : It was a green bonnet.

> *Camera cuts between them, the shots getting closer and closer.*

1ST WITNESS *shouting* : Red.

2ND WITNESS *shouting* : Green.

> *Camera cuts in even closer.*

1ST WITNESS *in an absolute fury* : Red.

2ND WITNESS *in as great a fury* : Green.

> *The* WITNESSES *try to shout one another down. The* DETECTIVE *looks on amazed. Intercut extreme close-up of both* WITNESSES.

1ST WITNESS : Red.

2ND WITNESS : Green.

1ST WITNESS : Red.

2ND WITNESS : Green.

1ST WITNESS : Red.

2ND WITNESS : Green.

> *The typist gets up. Group shot.*

DETECTIVE : Stop, stop ! . . . It's hopeless. Thank you, gentlemen.

1ST WITNESS : Of course, Inspector, if you are prepared to listen to a socialist . . .

> *Cut back to the office of the* CHIEF OF POLICE, *who is on the telephone again.*

CHIEF OF POLICE : The police have followed up, by today, more than fifteen hundred clues in this case. The dossiers we have collected fill sixty thick volumes. We have put all our men onto it . . .

> *Camera cuts to a medium close-up of several policemen beating through the undergrowth of a wood. The voice of the* CHIEF OF POLICE *continues over the following scenes.*

CHIEF OF POLICE *off* : . . . to systematically comb all the areas around the town . . . Every thicket, every piece of undergrowth, every clearing is carefully examined, because behind each bush . . .

> *Medium close-up of several policemen searching a*

wooded pit.

CHIEF OF POLICE *off* : . . . in every hole, we might find something that would put us at last on the right track . . .

Medium shot of a police dog as he picks up a scent and follows it to the edge of a lake, barking. A policeman follows him, holding him on a long leash. Other handlers and their dogs appear.

CHIEF OF POLICE *off* : . . . We have sent out police dogs. The best trackers have been put onto the weak scents we have found . . . without any result. Since this murderer's first crime . . .

Long shot of detectives checking the papers of down-and-outs in a scruffy dormitory of a doss-house, where rows of beds face one another and old clothing hangs from the walls.

CHIEF OF POLICE *off* : . . . the police have inspected all the doss-houses every night and checked the identity of every vagrant. Of course, these steps don't increase the popularity of the police, nor do they calm the nerves of the general public . . .

A smoky railway station. Detectives are checking everyone's papers.

CHIEF OF POLICE *off* : . . . Nevertheless, we are keeping up our watch on all railway stations. But these checks are no more successful than our nightly raids . . .

A deserted street at night lit by street lamps. A plainclothes policeman is accosted by a tart, but he goes on his way. Further on, under a street lamp, another girl talks with a client.

CHIEF OF POLICE *off* : . . . of the various underworld hangouts.

Shot from above we see a dark street still wet from recent rain. A couple disappear into a seedy hotel. A detective, beneath a street lamp opposite, looks on.

Shot from above in a wider angle, the headlights of a car light up the walls. Some men leap from the car while it is still moving and station themselves rapidly in various doorways. Their footsteps continue to echo over this and the following shots.

Three detectives are waiting in one doorway. One of them looks at his watch and gestures at the others. They move out of sight.

Shot from above we see the street with the seedy hotel. Three detectives can be seen coming out of a near-by doorway; one of them gives a signal: a whistle blows.

Shot from above we see two lorries full of men drive up. Policemen jump from cars. Motor-cycle policemen wait on their machines by the kerb. (Still on page 4) In the distance a group of plain-clothes men arrive, followed by uniformed men drawn up in two ranks. (Still on page 4)

Cut to a shot looking down over the roofs at a line of uniformed policemen and a group of detectives.

A young prostitute rushes into a sordid basement bar down the spiral staircase which leads from the street. It is an underworld hangout. A stuffed crocodile hangs from the ceiling and there is an old piano on the right.

PROSTITUTE : Cops! *(Still on page 21)*

Without wasting a second, the clients, criminals and whores, rush for the exit, scrambling over the tables and chairs. Seen from the exit, the landlady lowers a grille which shuts her off behind the bar. Everyone rushes for the stairs.

General chaos and confusion, seen in a high-angle shot looking down the empty staircase. The young prostitute appears first, followed by a thief who gives a sudden start and, furious, turns back. Others pass him to be turned back in their turn.

Police whistle. Car horns. A line of policemen, advancing steadily, pushes the fleeing crowd back down into the room.

Cut to the street: two plain-clothes men lead away a prostitute.

POLICEMAN'S VOICE : Police. Get back there.

YOUNG PROSTITUTE'S VOICE *among other cries*: Let me go, you bastard. Let me go. Eh, Inspector, let me go.

A policeman descends the stairs carrying the YOUNG PROSTITUTE *in his arms. The camera tracks with them*

34

and stops at the bottom of the stairs, beneath the arch of the entrance.

YOUNG PROSTITUTE : Let me go, won't you? . . . you beast, let me go, let me go. (*Still on page 22*)

THIEF : Let the girl alone, filthy copper.

General hubbub rising to a crescendo.

POLICE : Silence . . . silence !

The camera looks towards the stairs over the heads of the crowd, where a sergeant appears.

THE CROWD : Ah, the head cop. *Laughter.*

With a gesture the SERGEANT *commands silence.*

SERGEANT : Quiet.

A VOICE : That would suit you, wouldn't it?

The camera tilts down the stairs in the dim light of the cellar with the crowd of thieves and whores in the background; in the foreground, the dark silhouette of the SERGEANT.

SERGEANT : Police orders. Nobody leaves this place . . . Get your papers ready.

Cries of protest and whistles from around the room. The SERGEANT *stands in the entrance flanked on either side by police. An inspector comes down the stairs with one of his men. It is* INSPECTOR LOHMANN. *He stops on the bottom step, his face still in darkness.*

A VOICE : Let's see you, let's see you !

LOHMANN *cheerfully* : Come on now, children. Let's not do anything silly.

A THIEF *raising his hat* : It's fatty Lohmann.

A VOICE *chanting* : Loh-mann, Loh-mann, Loh-mann.

ANOTHER VOICE : Pop Lohmann !

Several wave their hats.

EVERYONE *in chorus* : Loh-mann ! Loh-mann ! Loh-mann !

The chanting ends in whistles. INSPECTOR LOHMANN *comes down the last step and enters the light. He is a strong looking man, about forty. He gives the impression of shrewd efficiency.*

LOHMANN : Quiet !

A VOICE : Get out !

LOHMANN : You'll wear yourself out.

A Woman's Voice *hysterically*: It would be better if you caught the child murderer.

Another Woman's Voice: Yes . . . much better! *Whistles.*

Lohmann: Quiet! Be reasonable!

He steps forward. Several policemen follow him.

Lohmann: Spread out . . . spread out all of you. All of you . . . spread out. Come on, come on now. Get your papers out.

More detectives come down the stairs.

A Voice: I haven't got any.

Lohmann *off*: Show me your papers.

A Girl *off, begging*: Let me go, please, Inspector.

One of the criminals is hiding at the back of the cloakroom. He tries to get out through a skylight, but suddenly starts back. Shot from below, through the grille of the skylight which gives onto the street: a policeman stands outside. The thief resignedly turns away.

In the ladies' toilet, a policeman enters, hesitates, then pulls back a curtain. A thief, embarrassed, comes out of his hiding place.

In the main cellar. Lohmann and two of his men are installed behind two tables. In front of him stands a young prostitute. Uniformed police form a corridor leading to the exit. In the background, the various occupants of the club are standing about.

Lohmann: Have you got any papers?

The Girl: But, Inspector, I can't go around everywhere with the date of my birth on me. That's asking too much.

Lohmann *indifferent*: Let's not beat around the bush, darling.

Reverse shot of Lohmann and one of his assistants; between them facing the camera, The Girl stands beside an enormous thug, with a black eye, wearing a cap, a fag-end in his mouth, hands in pockets. A row of police lines the wall.

The Girl *indignantly*: That's really asking too much, Inspector.

Lohmann *severely*: Alex*.

---

* Alex is short for Alexanderplatz, the headquarters of the Berlin police.

36

THE GIRL : Look here, it's disgusting.

She goes off to the right. Pushed by the others, the THUG *steps forward. He takes out a wallet and, very sure of himself, hands his papers to* LOHMANN. *Medium close-up of* LOHMANN *as he flicks through the papers. Sceptically, he examines their owner. Reverse shot of a policeman as he searches the* THUG. LOHMANN *whistles the song:* 'Where did you get your beautiful blue eyes?' *and looks at the* THUG *with an understanding look. Behind them, a group of thieves surrounded by police. The policeman finishes searching and goes out. The* THUG *puts his hands back in his pockets and looks at* LOHMANN *triumphantly. Medium close-up of* LOHMANN. *He smiles and holds the papers up to the light.*

LOHMANN *commiserating* : Poor workmanship, old boy. *Camera cuts quickly to the* THUG, *surprised; he takes his cigarette butt out of his mouth.* You've been had. *A pause. He signals to a policeman.* Alex.

The THUG *furiously throws his butt to the floor.*

THIEF *insolently* : Better luck next time, Willi.

THUG : Oh . . . you . . . shut your face.

LOHMANN : Next.

A greasy Mediterranean type steps forward, very smooth. He is wearing a sumptuous fur-collared overcoat. Taking off his bowler, he greets LOHMANN *obsequiously and presents his papers.*

ANOTHER THIEF *admiringly* : Fancy boy.

Another whistles. INSPECTOR LOHMANN *looks at the papers and gives them back. The* MAN *raises his hat again and prepares to leave. The camera tracks with him. Suddenly* LOHMANN *catches him with the handle of his walking stick and pulls him back.*

THE MAN *astonished* : What's the matter?

A THIEF : Pop Lohmann has got him.

SEVERAL VOICES : He's got him.

LOHMANN *takes a newspaper out of the* MAN'S *pocket and unfolds it. Shot of the front page of the newspaper dated 21st November, 1930. An illustrated article has been circled in pencil. It reads:* 'Unsolved burglary at *a furrier's shop.'* LOHMANN *puts down the paper.*

LOHMANN : Well . . . I think I had better take you down to headquarters.

THE MAN *horrified* : But after all, my . . . my papers are in order.

While he protests, his papers are taken from him.

LOHMANN : Next.

The next to come forward is a little fat man, cheerful and very friendly.

LITTLE FAT MAN *passing the smooth crook* : No luck, eh?

He comes up to the INSPECTOR, *and clumsily takes off his hat.*

LOHMANN : Next. *Holding out his hand.* Papers.

LITTLE FAT MAN *in a friendly tone* : I haven't got any.

LOHMANN : Alex.

LITTLE FAT MAN *shrugging his shoulders*: No luck. *He leaves.*

LOHMANN : Next . . . come on, let's carry on.

Two policeman search a corner of the room. They look under the tables, tip up the chairs and go through the pockets of the coats in the cloakroom. One finds a revolver, the other a leather brief-case. Close-up of the brief-case as it is opened: inside a complete house-breaking kit.

Things that have been confiscated are piled up, a jemmy, a saw, revolver bullets, etc. A hand adds the empty brief-case to the pile. The camera pans over the spread-out weapons towards the LANDLADY, *who stands behind her bar talking to a* SERGEANT, *who takes out a cigarette. Medium shot of them both.*

LANDLADY : This is ruining our business, Sergeant . . . Every night there's interference. No one can have ten minutes in peace anymore. Give us a chance !

She goes to the back of the bar and pours herself a drink. Close-up of the SERGEANT *lighting his cigarette at a gas lamp.*

SERGEANT : It's no joke for us either, out every night.

LANDLADY *in medium close-up* : Of course . . . but you're driving away my clientèle . . . And the fellow you're looking for isn't here. *She drinks.* You can't imagine how furious

38

everyone is about this guy who's causing a raid every night. Especially the girls . . . okay, they walk the streets . . . but, believe me, each one is a little bit of a mother.

The SERGEANT *leans on the bar surrounded by clouds of cigarette smoke, seen slightly from below.*

LANDLADY *off* : I know a lot of crooks. *Cut back to her . . .* who grow quite tender when they see kids playing. If they catch that bastard. *She makes a short, sharp gesture.* They'll wring his neck. *Close-up of them both.* Believe me.

Another policeman comes up and salutes the SERGEANT.

POLICEMAN : Ready to go, Sergeant?

The SERGEANT *touches the peak of his cap and leaves with the policeman.*

SERGEANT : Good night.

The LANDLADY *watches them leave with a gesture of disgust.*

Medium close-up of a man in plus-fours standing by the window of a comfortably furnished middle-class room; he is looking at the street through binoculars. He is a PICK-POCKET. *Quick tilt down to the street as two police lorries drive past, full of crooks.* INSPECTOR LOHMANN *follows in an open car. Cut back to the* PICK-POCKET *still looking through his binoculars.*

PICK-POCKET : So it's ' The Crocodile ' tonight. *He lowers the binoculars.* Two loads for the nick.

He turns round. On the sofa, smoking a cigarette, sits a tall, thin man. He is a CON-MAN, *dressed impeccably but a little pretentiously. He wears a dark jacket, a waist-coat and light trousers, and he has a thin moustache. Lounging beside him, a* BURGLAR, *tough but not very bright. He is also smoking. The* CON-MAN *gets up impatiently.*

CON-MAN : What's keeping Schränker?

Medium close-up and very slight tilt up to show the profile of a man with a moustache. He is a SAFE-BREAKER. *He is seated at the table in the centre of the room, playing cards.*

SAFE-BREAKER : Isn't it three o'clock yet?

PICK-POCKET : I'll find out.

He puts down the binoculars and walks from the window to the telephone in the middle of the room. Camera pans with him. He dials a number.

PICK-POCKET: Hello . . . The exact time, please, Miss. *He sits on the edge of the table.* Two minutes to three. Thank you.

He hangs up and, from various pockets, takes out a series of watches. He compares the time they show and places them on the table. Pan right onto the CON-MAN, *who has sat down beside him and is playing cards.*

PICK-POCKET *setting one of the watches*: Two minutes to three.

CON-MAN *disgusted*: There are more police on the streets than tarts.

Medium close-up of the BURGLAR *in an armchair, a bag under his arm. In the foreground, in front of him, a small low table, with an ashtray on it overflowing with dog-ends.*

BURGLAR: Wherever you spit . . . nothing but cops.

The SAFE-BREAKER, *chewing on his cigarette holder, comes up to the table. He wears a white waistcoat and a white bow-tie. The camera tracks back: a 1900 style chandelier comes into shot.*

PICK-POCKET: Even when you're with a doll, they don't leave you in peace . . . And they've gone nuts too . . . All they can think about is that murderer . . . *To the* SAFE-BREAKER . . . Mine . . . she's got a little six-year old girl, and, every night, I have to waste time searching under the bed and in the cupboards to make sure the murderer isn't hiding there.

The CON-MAN *spreads three cards out on the table. The* SAFE-BREAKER *indicates a card with the look of an expert. The* CON-MAN *turns it up. It is an ace. The* PICK-POCKET *takes out a handkerchief and spreads it out beside the watches.*

PICK-POCKET: You can't even get on with your job. Everywhere you come across the police. There's no privacy any more . . . I'm fed up.

The camera tracks back to show the SAFE-BREAKER *walking round the table, looking at the time as he passes.*

40

Con-Man *bored* : Tell us something new.

He puts the cards in his pocket. The Pick-pocket *arranges his watches in the handkerchief and slips them into his pocket. The* Safe-Breaker *sits down again.*

Con-Man : What's keeping Schränker?

Pick-pocket : Maybe he's been caught.

Burglar *laughing* : Not him. *He rejoins the others.* He did a bank job in London and Scotland Yard set a trap for him . . . there he was, hands up, back to the wall, millions of cops all round . . . and two seconds later there were two bodies on the ground and he'd scarpered!

The Burglar *has sat down, his bag on his knee. The* Safe-Breaker *lights another cigarette from the stub of the first.*

Safe-Breaker *with respect* : The best man between Berlin and San Francisco.

Burglar : They've been looking for him for six years and they haven't caught him.

Pick-pocket *ironically* : Haven't caught him . . . Dogs kill wolves.

Safe-Breaker : Shut up.

The Pick-pocket *tries to calm the* Safe-Breaker. *They are all nervous and worried, and smoke heavily. The* Con-Man *looks at the time again.*

Con-Man : The suspense is killing. He's usually bang on time.

On these last words, the door bell rings four times. Relieved, they look at one another.

Pick-pocket : God be praised!

Burglar : At last!

The door opens. Schranker *appears in leather overcoat, bowler hat and carrying a walking stick. He immediately shuts the door, but doesn't come into the room.*

All : Good afternoon . . . You've got here at last. Good afternoon.

Schranker : Are you mad? Close the curtains.

Cut to the window showing the curtains half-drawn. Next to it is the table where the Safe-Breaker *is sitting. The* Pick-pocket *creeps along the wall to the window to avoid being seen from the street. From above we see*

45

the PICK-POCKET *returning to his place at the table in the middle of the room.* SCHRANKER *comes over to him and takes off his hat, putting it on the table with his stick.*

SCHRANKER: Gentlemen, the meeting can now begin. *He takes off his overcoat to reveal a chalk-stripe suit, dark tie and black leather gloves. He sits down to preside over the meeting.* According to the regulations, I confirm with pleasure that the leadership of every organisation in our Union is represented. *He grasps his stick.* I assume that you all have full powers . . .

> *Medium close-up of the* SAFE-BREAKER, *who nods. Pan to the* PICK-POCKET, *who is cracking a nut; he nods too, then to the* CON-MAN *who, while lighting a cigarette, also nods. Finally, the* BURGLAR, *still bent over the bag, also gives his assent.*

SCHRANKER *off*: . . . authorizing you to vote for your members. Good . . . let's not be held up by procedure. *Reverse shot of the whole group.* We all know why we are here. *Vehemently.* Someone who is not a member of the Union is messing up our affairs. The new measures taken by the police, the daily raids in our areas to find this child murderer, interfere with our business activities in a quite unbearable way. We can put up no longer with the endless pressure from the police, in every hotel, café, or flat.

SAFE-BREAKER: Quite right.

PICK-POCKET: Here, here!

SCHRANKER: This state of affairs must not be allowed to continue. We'll have to put things right again or we'll be destroyed.

> *Medium close-up of the* BURGLAR, *who stubs out his cigarette. As* SCHRANKER *continues to talk, the* BURGLAR *takes out another cigarette and strikes a match. Now and again* SCHRANKER'S *gloved hand, playing with his stick, passes across frame.*

SCHRANKER *off*: The funds of our organization are exhausted. Unless I make use of the funds put aside to support the wives of our colleagues who are being looked after by the state, I just don't know where I'll find the funds needed for

46

the preparation and execution of our various projects. What is more, our reputation is suffering. *Big close-up of* SCHRANKER. . . . The cops are looking for the murderer in our ranks, gentlemen . . . When I come up against a cop while carrying on my business, he knows the risk he runs . . . and I do, as well. If one of us dies . . . okay . . . that's a risk one must take. It can happen: but we are not on the same level as this man they're looking for now.

> *From behind* SCHRANKER *and over his head can be seen the rest of the group.* SCHRANKER *has underlined his last words with a wide gesture.*

SAFE-BREAKER: Exactly.

SCHRANKER: There is an abyss between him and us.

BURGLAR: Of course.

PICK-POCKET *at the same time*: No comparison.

SCHRANKER *off*: We are doing our job. . . *Close-up of him* . . . because we have a living to make. But this monster has no right to live. He must dis . . . app . . . ear. He must be exterminated, without pity . . . without scruples. *Camera cuts to a high shot of* SCHRANKER *facing the group.* Gentlemen, our members must be able to carry on their business normally, without being handicapped by the growing nervousness of the police. I'm appealing to you . . . *He invites comments; on his gesture, the camera cuts to the* . . .

> CHIEF OF POLICE *who continues* SCHRANKER'S *same gesture. A meeting is also in progress at his office, and seen from above, policemen and high-ranking detective inspectors are sitting at a long conference table. It is littered with brandy glasses and coffee cups and the air is full of cigar-smoke. The* CHIEF OF POLICE *is standing at the head of the table, furthest from camera.*

CHIEF OF POLICE: . . . for advice.

> *He sits down and a police officer rises. Beside him a bespectacled man in plain clothes listens attentively.*

THE OFFICER *in a military tone*: I suggest a closer watch on identity cards, a systematic search of the whole town, police raids. *The bespectacled man looks dubious.* More numerous raids, and certainly tougher ones. *He sits down.*

> *Cut back to the underworld meeting, the* CON-MAN *gets*

up. He faces camera, beside him the BURGLAR. *To the left, in the foreground, is the* PICK-POCKET.

CON-MAN: Spies . . . We need spies in the ranks of the police to give us plenty of warning of new measures.

BURGLAR: The girls must take a little more notice of the cops. We're always getting into trouble because one of the girls has grassed to her cop boyfriend. *The* PICK-POCKET *agrees; the* CON-MAN *sits down satisfied.* Now, it's up to the girls to grass for us!

The SAFE-BREAKER *rises on the right, in the foreground is the* PICK-POCKET.

SAFE-BREAKER: What we must do . . . And after all, we've all got contacts . . . What we must do is make a statement to the Press ourselves, tell them that *we,* the Organization, members of the Union — *we* condemn the bastard just as much! We ought to make it known that the police should quit looking for him in the underworld.

Camera cuts back to the Police meeting where an elderly bespectacled detective, with a small beard and a stiff collar, is speaking. Another detective sits on his right; on his left, a police-officer with a monocle.

ELDERLY DETECTIVE: I'm sure it's a man who looks like a peaceful little family man, who wouldn't harm a fly, except when he has his fits, of course! *Medium close-up of* LOHMANN, *who listens with interest, as the* ELDERLY DETECTIVE *continues off* . . . Perhaps in his normal state, he even plays marbles with the concierge's children. LOHMANN *nods agreement* . . . Or perhaps plays cards with his wife. *Cut back to the* ELDERLY DETECTIVE. Without this appearance of, let's say inoffensiveness in private life, it would be impossible to believe that murderers like Grossmann or Haarmann were able to live for years in large, busy blocks of flats without their neighbours suspecting them in the slightest.

An OFFICER *with a moustache, smoking a pipe, agrees; beside him a plain-clothes man takes notes.*

THE OFFICER: That's what we must get across to the public. They must help.

Close-up of LOHMANN, *clearly annoyed, rising to his feet.*

LOHMANN: Don't talk to me about help from the general public. It disgusts me just to hear them talk. *He bows towards the* CHIEF OF POLICE. Excuse me, Chief . . . *Camera cuts quickly to the* CHIEF *who, smiling, makes a gesture accepting the apology* . . . Excuse me, but that is the truth. *Cut back to* LOHMANN. Good God! Has help from the public brought us one useful clue? *Furiously, he stubs out his cigar.* Just a pile of letters full of the most incredible accusations!

Camera cuts quickly to two INSPECTORS *at the end of the table.*

FIRST INSPECTOR : Quite true.

LOHMANN : Calls to the police as soon as a dustman crosses a yard.

SECOND INSPECTOR : Exactly.

LOHMANN : But when we want really accurate information . . . they can't remember anything, they have seen nothing. That's help from the public for you.

LOHMANN *leaves his place. Medium close-up of the* CHIEF OF POLICE.

CHIEF OF POLICE *smiling*: I think you exaggerate a little, Lohmann.

Cut back to the underworld meeting, great clouds of smoke drift over the table. They are all deep in thought. The PICK-POCKET *breaks the silence.*

PICK-POCKET : I've an idea! There's a magician, no, a tele . . . telepa . . . or is it radiologist? Anyway, I don't know what you call them . . . one of those guys who finds handkerchiefs and wallets that have been hidden.

Camera cuts back to a uniformed OFFICER *speaking at the Police meeting. The last words from the* PICK-POCKET *overlay what he is saying.*

OFFICER : I also think the reward isn't high enough.

His neighbour, an INSPECTOR, *gestures in disagreement and gets up.*

OFFICER : Chief . . . we must offer a real fortune for catching the murderer.

The INSPECTOR *pushes his chair up to the table.*

INSPECTOR *irritably, as he leaves*: None of this is getting us anywhere.

Camera cuts back to show the crooks' meeting, slightly

from above. Clouds of cigarette smoke hang round the fringed lampshade.

SAFE-BREAKER : That won't do any good.

CON-MAN : Well, what do you suggest?

The BURGLAR *gets up, moves round behind his armchair and leans on the back of it.*

BURGLAR : All the same we can't just wait until the police make up their minds to arrest this fellow.

An INSPECTOR *with long disorderly white hair leans over the back of his chair towards* THE CHIEF OF POLICE, *continuing the movement of the* BURGLAR *as the camera cuts back to the police meeting. The* POLICEMAN *with the monocle sits on his left; on his right in the foreground, another* INSPECTOR *sits.*

THE INSPECTOR : The difficulty of solving this type of crime is increased by the fact that wrongdoer and the victim are only connected by a chance meeting. An instantaneous impulse is the killer's only motive.

THE CHIEF OF POLICE *impressed* : Hmm . . . Hmm.

THE INSPECTOR : We find the victim; we identify him; we find out when he was last seen . . . And then, and then, nothing more. The children disappear.

Cut back to a group shot of the underworld meeting where the SAFE-BREAKER *is standing on the left. In the background, the rest are seated round the table. The* BURGLAR *is perched on the back of his chair.*

SAFE-BREAKER : The police have been looking for this murderer for eight months now. Now it's got to the point where they'll only catch him by luck.

BURGLAR : We can't wait for that . . .

CON-MAN : We'll be ruined before then.

SAFE-BREAKER : What are we going to do then?

Cut back to a high group shot of the police meeting. The room is misty with thick clouds of smoke. The meeting has come to a full stop and some of the officers have got up and are pacing around the room.

Camera cuts again to the same high group shot of the underworld meeting, where the PICK-POCKET *has made a huge question mark with the shells of his nuts on the*

table. (Still on page 23) The Safe-Breaker *and the* Burglar *both pace restlessly up and down.*
Cut back to a high shot from above of the police conference table. We can see that most people have left their places and are wandering around the room.
Cut back to the underworld meeting, only the Pick-Pocket *and* Schranker *are seated. The* Con-Man *stands by the table, and the* Safe-Breaker *has moved into the background by the window.*

Schranker *decisively* : We'll have to catch him ourselves.
The others gather round him.

All : Yes . . . we must. This is what we must do.
Lohmann's *voice is heard over as the camera cuts back to show abandoned chairs round the conference table with most of the delegates wandering up and down. But gradually their attention is drawn by what* Lohmann *is saying, and one or two nod their heads in agreement.*

Lohmann *off* : There is still one possible way. The guilty man or the possible suspects must already have a record somewhere. Such a person, deeply disturbed, must already have fallen foul of the law. We've got to contact every clinic, every prison, every lunatic asylum. *Noise of general agreement.* We'll have to make enquiries about everyone who has been freed as harmless but who has the same pathological condition as the killer.
Camera cuts to a close-up, followed by an extreme close-up to Schranker's *black-gloved hand placed over a map of the town. (Still on page 23)*

Schranker *off* : Every square yard must be permanently watched. From now on no child must take a step without us being warned.

Con-Man : Okay, but how do we do it?
Safe-Breaker : Yes . . . how?
Schranker *off* : There must be people . . . *The group is seen silhouetted in shadow on the wall,* Schranker's *shadow in the centre* . . . who can go anywhere without being noticed . . . who can follow anyone on the streets without arousing suspicion . . . who can follow the children right to their front doors without any trouble. In fact, people no one would

51

suspect of being guilty. (*Still on page 24*)

THE OTHERS *off* : But who? . . . Who? People like that don't exist . . . Who could do it? . . . Who? . . . Who?

Schranker pauses and then rises so that his shadow on the wall swells up.

SCHRANKER *off* : The beggars. The beggars' union.

In the foreground at the Beggars' Market, the camera pans onto a notice which reads: NO MORE CREDIT. The camera pans, then tracks towards a table where two beggars are laying out bits of bread and slices of sausage. The tracking continues and ends in a close-up of their hands with the bread and sausage.

1ST BEGGAR *off*: Sausage going up.

2ND BEGGAR *off* : God, this cheese smells good.

Pan across to another table where a game of cards is in progress. Only the players' hands and the cards are visible.

3RD BEGGAR *off* : That finishes you.

Pan up to show a grizzled tramp, who has brought in a live chicken. He finishes a glass of wine. Camera tracks on past a grille in front of a cloakroom and comes to rest on another tramp, snoring. Beside him, two others take the fillings out of sandwiches.

4TH BEGGAR : Stop snoring! You'll wake the lice.

The camera tracks in towards the counter where the fat Boss of the Beggars' Market takes a steaming sausage out of a pot and takes a bite. Then he counts a packet of sandwiches one of them has brought him.

THE BOSS *counting* : Two, four, six, eight, ten, twelve, fourteen, sixteen, eighteen, twenty, twenty-two, twenty-four, twenty-six . . .

As he continues, the camera rises towards a huge blackboard fixed to the wall behind him. On it is written ' PRICES FOR THE EVENING OF THE 16th,' and then a list of every sort of sandwich, classified according to filling and the quality of the bread. The Boss gets up on a stool and alters certain prices, murmuring to himself.

BOSS : Sandwiches : Friday, bad day for cold meat . . . No go.

52

The voice continues, as the camera pans up to the floor above where there is a strange sort of office. A vulture's skeleton is on the left in the foreground. At the back of the room, beggars form a queue. (Still on page 24) Camera tracks through the window towards the office where two men from the Beggar's Union are working. One is studying a map of the town, the other is writing names into a huge register.

1st Man : Now, we must deal with the back-yards.

2nd Man : Yes, from number one to number forty-eight.

Camera tracks towards Schranker *who leans against the wall watching the work. Pan towards a door with a glass panel on which can be read:* ACCOUNTS. Please give your name to the outside office.

In the corridor, as in the office, beggars wait behind a small barrier.

2nd Man *off* : Next.

The pan continues, as the barrier is raised and a beggar comes up, taking off his cap. Shot of the Two Men, *the* Beggar *standing in front of them, his back to the camera; he is given a small slip of paper. The* 2nd Man *keeps a carbon copy of it.*

2nd Man : You are responsible for the courtyards of every block of flats from 1 to 81 High Street.

Beggar : Right.

The Beggar *goes out. Another comes up.*

2nd Man : Next.

Insert of a street map marked with the places where the children have disappeared and been murdered. Close-up of the 1st Man's *pencil which follows one of the streets.*

1st Man *off* : 89 to 196 High Street . . . Fine.

Camera cuts back to a medium shot of the office. One tramp stands with his back to the camera and two more join him. The 2nd Man *notes down the first one's particulars.*

2nd Man *writing* : 89 to 196 High Street . . . What's your union number?

Tramp *after some thought* : Three, seven, ninety-five. Emil Dustermann.

Large close-up of a hand writing the name and number in the register.

2ND MAN: Three . . . seven . . . ninety-five . . . Emil Dustermann . . .

The hand tears a slip from the register. Shot from above of a line of BEGGARS *with* DUSTERMANN *in the foreground: he has a wooden leg and leans on a stick . . .*

2ND MAN: There you are, Emil. *He gives him the paper.* Maybe, you'll win the fifteen thousand.

DUSTERMANN *tapping his leg*: Touch wood.

Camera cuts to another part of the market where an assorted collection of second-hand goods and junk is on display. A line of metal grilles form a cash desk, and there are violins and accordions spread out on a long table. In the background there are several barrel organs, and on a shelf a stack of old shoes and boots. A constant murmur of voices reaches us from other parts of the market. The junk dealer is demonstrating one of the barrel organs to a beggar, but it is very out of key and only plays a few wheezy notes.

Medium close-up of the BLIND BEGGAR, *who sold a balloon to the* MURDERER. *He is sitting at a nearby table drinking a beer, balloons floating above him. Putting down his glass, he covers his ears. Immediately, the excruciating noise from the barrel organ stops; but as he lowers his hands, it starts up again. After a while another organ starts to play a polka. The* BLIND MAN *is delighted and conducts an imaginary orchestra.*

The music continues over as the camera cuts to a high shot of the courtyard of a tenement block. It is early evening and the setting sun casts long shadows across the tarmac. In the gloom a few children stand in twos and threes watching the BEGGAR *playing a barrel organ, and coins are thrown from windows above. (Still on page 41) Medium close-up of the barrel organ. The music stops and the last coin rolls along the ground.*

THE BEGGAR *off*: Thank you, ladies and gentlemen, thank you.

Camera cuts to another street, where a beggar's legs are

seen from above. The BEGGAR *is seated on the kerb, his hat upturned beside him. A man and a little girl pass, but only their legs are visible. The little girl throws a coin into the hat.*

Medium close-up of the BEGGAR *wearing dark glasses and a notice round his neck saying ' BLIND '. A German sheepdog sits beside him.*

BEGGAR : Thank you.

The two shadows of the passers-by draw away. The BEGGAR *lifts his glasses and takes a sly look after them, and the dog turns its head in the same direction. (Still on page 41) From the* BEGGAR'S *point-of-view, we see the man and the little girl walking off arm-in-arm. Camera follows them, past a poster advertising ' West-front 1918 '. The man goes with the little girl as far as the entrance to a school. He kisses her and leaves her there. Beside the school entrance, another* BEGGAR, *with two white pigeons, is on the look out. Camera cuts to two little girls looking into the window of a sweet shop.* EMIL DUSTERMANN *stands beside the window.*

Next we see into the window of a toy shop, where a windmill and a fairground roundabout are turning. Two children stop to watch while their nurse continues her walk. Other children join the first two, and there is a legless beggar, squatting on a little cart, looking on.

In his office, INSPECTOR LOHMANN, *is sitting at his desk, smoking a cigar and reading a letter. Insert of the type-written letter in the machine:* ' When searching their homes, we must above all look for any clue by which we could establish where the murderer's letter to the papers originated. If there is an old wooden table on which the letter could have been written, if there is a red pencil or any tiny pieces from sharpening such a pencil, or writing paper of the same type. The inquiries must be made as discreetly as possible.'

LOHMANN'S *hand comes into shot holding a pen. He underlines the words* ' old *wooden* table ' *and corrects a typing error.*

LOHMANN *muttering off* : Idiot. *He also underlines the words* 'red pencil'. *There is a knock on the door.* Come in.

The whole office comes into frame as LOHMANN *signs the letter. An* ASSISTANT *comes in and passes him a file.*

THE ASSISTANT: Here's the list of mental patients who have been let out as cured or harmless in the last five years.

Insert of the file as LOHMANN *sorts through it. It contains reports from ' Dr. Goll's Psychiatric Institute,' from ' Professor Emil Lebbowitz's private clinic for mental patients,' from ' The Protestant Hospital of Nazareth,' from ' The Elizabeth Clinic,' from ' St. Hedwig's Hospital,' etc.*

ASSISTANT *off*: Reports from every institute, private and public. LOHMANN *picks up another file* . . . And that's a list of their present addresses.

LOHMANN *opens the file and flicks through it.*

Camera cuts to the MURDERER, *coming out into the street from a lower middle-class rooming house and moving away to the left.* LOHMANN'S ASSISTANT *immediately appears from the right. He hesitates an instant, then throws down his cigarette and goes in.*

Close-up of a name plate above a bell. It reads: ELIZABETH WINKLER.

In the entrance hall, a close-up of the ASSISTANT'S *hand as he ruffles through a notebook full of addresses. All except the last three have been crossed out. His finger stops at* HANS BECKERT, c/o E. WINKLER, Gleder St. 15, 2nd Floor.

Dissolve to the ASSISTANT *standing by a door on the landing. He rings and puts his notebook away. A small, frightened old lady answers the door. A large key-ring is fixed to her apron. The* ASSISTANT *greets her. Shot of them both.*

MRS. WINKLER *very softly*: Morning.

ASSISTANT: Does a Mr. Beckert live here?

MRS. WINKLER *cups a hand round her ear to hear better.*

MRS. WINKLER: What?

ASSISTANT *louder*: Does Mr. Beckert live here?

MRS. WINKLER: I'm afraid I can't hear you . . . I'm a bit hard of hearing.

ASSISTANT *to one side*: As if I didn't know. *Shouting.* Does a Mr. Beckert live here?

MRS. WINKLER *a little worried*: Oh. Mr. Beckert? Yes . . . yes, of course. Yes, Mr. Beckert lives here. I'm afraid he has just gone out.

ASSISTANT: Pity . . . I wanted to see him.

MRS. WINKLER *very softly*: Oh, yes. *She shrugs her shoulders.*

ASSISTANT *loudly*: I'm from the Income Tax people.

MRS. WINKLER *startled*: Oh, good God! The tax people? Yes . . . yes. Would you like . . . would you like to wait?

She gestures to him to come in. He bows.

ASSISTANT: Yes, thank you.

MRS. WINKLER: Not at all, please take a seat.

She goes out. The ASSISTANT *puts his hat on the round central table and sits down. As soon as the door is closed, he jumps up to examine the room, but he hears* MRS. WINKLER *coming back and only just has time to sit down again. She hands him a newspaper.*

MRS. WINKLER: Perhaps you'd like something to read?

ASSISTANT *loudly*: Thank you. You're most kind.

MRS. WINKLER: Not at all.

He takes the paper. Close-up of the front page of the ' General Anzeiger' for 24th November, 1930.

ASSISTANT *off*: Tell me, Mrs. Winkler, does Mr. Beckert take this paper?

The ASSISTANT *sits in an armchair, his back to the camera.* MRS. WINKLER, *already at the door, turns round.*

MRS. WINKLER *astonished*: Mr. Beckert? *She laughs.* No, he always borrows mine.

ASSISTANT: Ah, thank you.

MRS. WINKLER *nods and leaves the room. As soon as she has closed the door again, the* ASSISTANT *gets up and looks at the table where he put his hat. He throws the hat onto a chair and carefully raises the cloth. From high overhead we see him bending over the table and scratching the wood with his finger nails.*

Cut to a medium close-up of a fruit-seller's barrow in the street, piled high with apples, oranges and bananas.

From a strut hang some superb pineapples. The MUR-
DERER *is standing behind the barrow dolefully eating an
apple, at the same time gesturing to the fruit-seller to
put another in the bag being filled for him.*
Back in the MURDERER'S *room still seen from above,
the* ASSISTANT *finishes his inspection; disappointed by
the negative search, he slowly replaces the cloth. Camera
cuts to a slight low shot of the* ASSISTANT *beside the
table. Above his head, hangs a Tiffany-style glass lampshade, and beyond him a large pottery stove stands
against the wall. As the* ASSISTANT *carefully surveys the
room, camera pans across from the bedside table to the
double windows. There is a bowl of fruit and other food-
stuffs stored in the space between them. We recognise
the same wide windowseat where the* MURDERER *wrote
his letter to the press. Pan continues until it reaches the*
ASSISTANT *again. He is leaning over a wicker wastepaper basket from which he extracts an empty cigarette
packet, a publicity hand-out for cigars and a postcard,
which he lifts up and studies carefully.*
Cut to the street: the MURDERER *is eating an apple and
looking at a window display in a cutlery and silverware
shop. We see him from inside through the glass, his face
framed in the reflection of a diamond-shaped display of
knives. The reflection of other cutlery form geometric
patterns around him. (Still on page 42)*
*Camera cuts back to show the street behind him and
his view of the shop window: the knives are arranged
round a diamond-shaped mirror on the screen at the
back of the window.*
Close-up of the MURDERER *munching his apple. Suddenly
he stops chewing. Reflected in the mirror he can see a
little girl leaning against the railings on the other
side of the street, the image framed with knives. The*
MURDERER *stands transfixed, staring at her. He wipes
his mouth with the back of his hand, eyes bulging. The
little girl leans nonchalantly on the railings, obviously
waiting for someone. The* MURDERER'S *arms fall limply
to his side, he gasps for breath and his eyes close as he*

58

sways forward against the shop front. Then the fit sub-sides and he recovers slightly. Seen in reflection, the little girl leaves the railings and goes out of sight. The MURDERER *wheels round and follows her with his eyes. He lowers his head and sets off slowly, whistling the 'Peer Gynt' theme.*

In the MURDERER'S *room, the* ASSISTANT *picks up an empty sweet carton from the bedside table, examines it and makes a note. Camera cuts back to the same street to a view of a bookshop window, where a cardboard circle with a spiral design turns endlessly while a huge arrow shoots endlessly up an down. The little girl stares fascinated by the continual motion, until she turns away distracted by something else. The 'Peer Gynt' theme accompanies her, whistled piercingly, as camera follows her as she wanders on past other shop windows. Suddenly she turns delightedly and flings her arms round a smart young woman who has come into shot from the right. The whistling stops abruptly. The woman and the little girl walk off, arms round each other. Camera follows them along the pavement as they pass the* MURDERER *who ducks into the doorway of the bookshop, back to camera, pretending to look at some books displayed there. He looks round furtively and eventually steps out into the street to watch them go, his eyes drooping and his mouth partly open. He puts his hands together on his chest, nervously scratching them. Behind him the arrow continues to fly up and down, appearing to pierce the revolving spiral at every descent. The* MURDERER *scratches the back of his hand nervously.*

The camera follows the MURDERER *as he turns into a café with tables outside, screened from the street by a trellis of climbing plants. He sits at a table to the left of the opening, his face just visible in profile through the foliage. A* WAITER *comes out to serve him.*

WAITER : Good evening . . . What would you like?

MURDERER : Coffee.

WAITER *bending nearer* : Sorry?

MURDERER *controlling himself* : No . . . a vermouth . . . No, a brandy.

The WAITER *bows and withdraws.*

MURDERER *exhausted*: Brandy . . . brandy . . .

The camera tracks in towards the foliage. The MURDERER *starts to whistle and then takes out a cigarette as the* WAITER'S *hand pours a brandy.*

WAITER: There you are.

The MURDERER *drinks the brandy in a gulp. The glass rings against the table, as he puts it down.*

MURDERER *in a broken voice*: Another one.

The WAITER'S *hand pours another glass.*

WAITER: There.

The MURDERER *swallows the second glass, leans forward and stares fixedly in front of him. With a mechanical gesture he puts a cigarette in his mouth and immediately takes it out again. He presses his two bunched fists into his eyes and starts to whistle again. Then he covers his ears. In the background the lights of the café come on and faintly light up the table. He immediately stops whistling and gets up. We track away from him rapidly.*

MURDERER: The bill.

WAITER *coming up*: Two brandies. One sixty-five please. *Coins fall on the saucer.* Thanks very much.

The MURDERER *departs whistling, his hands in his pockets.*

Cut to LOHMANN, *in his office, an enormous cigar in his hand. He sits at his desk thinking. Beside him, his* ASSISTANT *makes his report.*

ASSISTANT: Number 24: Beckert. He does not take the *Stadtischer Courier.* A walnut table with a cloth. No red pencil, nor any traces of such a pencil. No writing paper. In the wastepaper basket, a printed advertisement and a coloured postcard . . . *Medium close-up of* LOHMANN *thinking: behind him we see a map of the town* . . . of a bunch of flowers. Written on it: ' Regards, Paul.' No address of sender. An empty cigarette packet, Ariston brand. A bag of sweets with the name of a sweet shop . . .

LOHMANN *interrupting him*: Wait . . . wait a moment. *He screws up his eyes and thinks.* Ariston, did you say? *Track in.*

A . . . ris . . . ton. *Track in. Deep in thought he writes the name in the air. Camera tracks in closer.*

LOHMANN : That rings a bell . . . Ariston. *Camera tracks in even closer. Suddenly,* LOHMANN *seems to have got it. He grabs the telephone.* Hello. I want the file on the Marga Perl murder. Straightaway.

He hangs up. Camera cuts to the blind balloon seller's kiosk, where the BLIND MAN *has just sold two balloons to a woman who pays and goes off.*

BLIND MAN : Thank you very much.

From far off, we hear the MURDERER'S *whistling approach. His shadow passes. The* BLIND MAN *lifts his head.*

BLIND MAN : That's funny . . . I've heard that somewhere before. *Camera draws in closer.* It was . . . it was . . .

The BLIND MAN *walks forward tapping with his stick. Camera tracks back in front of him. Astonished passersby watch him wave. Pan across a very busy street. In the foreground, some planks half cover a hole in the road. The* BLIND MAN, *still holding some balloons, comes up to it.*

BLIND MAN : Hey, hey, Henry.

A young man in a cap pops up immediately. Medium close-up of them both.

HENRY : What is it?

He takes the BLIND MAN'S *hand.*

BLIND MAN : Listen a moment. There's someone whistling. Can't you hear him?

HENRY *cocks his head and cups his ear. Their two faces turn in the direction of the whistling.*

BLIND MAN : There.

HENRY *listens. But the whistling suddenly stops.*

BLIND MAN : He's just stopped . . . Did you see him, the guy who was whistling?

HENRY : Yes, yes, I can still see him.

BLIND MAN : Yes?

HENRY : Sure. *Excited.* He's talking to a little girl as he walks down the street with her.

BLIND MAN : After him and don't let him go.

65

HENRY: But why?

BLIND MAN: The day Elsie Beckmann was killed someone bought a balloon off me. He was with a little girl . . . HENRY *rushes off* . . . and the fellow whistled just like that!

HENRY *runs to the end of the roadworks and looks round. Camera follows him, as he enters a quiet street running at right angles to the previous one. In a basement a greengrocer's shop is lit up. He approaches and looks through the window. Camera cuts to a view through the window from above. The* MURDERER *and the* LITTLE GIRL *are being served by an old woman. She hands them a big paper bag and some sweets for the girl, who thanks her as the* MURDERER *pays. Camera cuts back to* HENRY *in the street, in front of the window; he stands up and hesitates for a moment. Taking one last look through the window, he runs off to the right out of shot. Camera now cuts to show him hiding in a corner of the roadworks between the tar boiler and a great roll of cable. He watches the street.*

The MURDERER *and the* LITTLE GIRL *come out of the shop. She offers him the bag of fruit and he takes an orange. Anxiously, he looks right and left, but there is no one in sight. Then he sweeps back his coat and puts his hand into his trouser pocket. Huge close-up as he takes out a flick knife. The blade glints and flashes in the gloom.*

Quick cut to show HENRY *ready to jump out.*

Return in close-up of the blade peeling an orange. Camera cuts back again to show HENRY, *who is searching his pockets; he takes out a piece of chalk. Large close-up of the palm of* HENRY'S *left hand on which he draws a large letter M.*

Cut back to the MURDERER, *facing the girl, his back to camera. He finishes peeling his orange and throws the peel onto the ground.* HENRY *comes up, hurriedly. As though by mistake, he knocks against the* MURDERER *and so gets a chance to place his left hand against the* MURDERER'S *shoulder. Terrified, the* MURDERER *backs away, dropping the knife.*

66

HENRY *feigning annoyance*: Damn it, are you crazy, throwing your peel on the ground? *He shrugs his shoulders and goes out of frame. Off:* I might have broken my neck. Unbelievable.

Close-up of the knife on the ground, then back to show the whole scene.

HENRY: I should report you to the police . . . You're a danger to the public.

The LITTLE GIRL *picks up the knife, gets up and hands it to the* MURDERER. *Camera rises with her and frames them both in profile. The* LITTLE GIRL *gives the still shaken* MURDERER *a little nudge. (Still on page 43)*

LITTLE GIRL: Uncle.

The MURDERER *takes the knife as the camera circles round behind him, to show, high on his back, an M outlined in chalk.*

Cut to INSPECTOR LOHMANN'S *office, where* LOHMANN *sits at his desk, his* ASSISTANT *standing beside him.* LOHMANN *studies a dossier, following the lines with his finger. Suddenly he raises his head.*

LOHMANN: There . . . that's it. They found three cigarette stubs where the crime took place — Aristons.

ASSISTANT: Yes, the cigarettes are the same, but there is no old wooden table.

Nervously, LOHMANN *waves away the objection and plunges back into the dossier, while his* ASSISTANT *faces the window.*

ASSISTANT *thoughtfully*: Of course . . . he could have written the letter somewhere else, but . . . *Suddenly he leans towards* LOHMANN . . . Heavens, the windowsill!

Large close-up of the windowsill in the MURDERER'S *room. A hand holding a magnifying glass comes into shot. Through the magnifying glass in huge close-up, we see the grain of the wood.* LOHMANN *and his* ASSISTANT *closely examine the windowsill.* LOHMANN *holds the magnifying glass and we see them in profile.*

LOHMANN: You're right!

ASSISTANT *opening one of the windows*: Just a minute!

He bends over the gap between the double windows and

*pushes a wet finger into it. Then he examines the bits of
dust. Large close-up of his dirty finger.*

ASSISTANT : A red pencil!

LOHMANN *and his* ASSISTANT *stand in front of the
window.*

LOHMANN : Good God . . . At last, we are getting somewhere!
Cut to SCHRANKER *sitting with his back to the camera,
in the room where the underworld meeting was held.
He is wearing his bowler. The* SAFE-BREAKER *is on the
telephone opposite him. The* BURGLAR *and the* PICK-
POCKET *are standing beside him. They all wear overcoats.*

SAFE-BREAKER *into the telephone* : Yes . . . yes . . . What?
To the others : They're on his trail.

CON-MAN *off* : They've found him?

PICK-POCKET : The beggars found him.

BURGLAR : He was talking to a little girl.

CON-MAN : Tell me more.

PICK-POCKET : They put a mark on him.

SAFE-BREAKER : Can't you be quiet? *Into the telephone.*
What's that?

Medium close-up of HENRY *in a telephone kiosk.*

HENRY *into the telephone* : They are following the sign. They
are not letting him out of their sight for a second.

The MURDERER *walks slowly down a street with the*
LITTLE GIRL. *They go out of shot. A passer-by throws
down a cigarette end. A tramp comes up, picks up the
stub and follows the* MURDERER; *he is accompanied by
a colleague with one leg.*

New shot of the MURDERER *and the* LITTLE GIRL, *as
they reach a column covered with posters. The two*
BEGGARS *follow close behind. The* ONE-LEGGED MAN
*disappears behind the column and a man in a cap
takes his place. The* BEGGAR *jerks up one thumb.*

*Dissolve to a view of the street, shot through a half-open
door. Behind the door is the outline of a man on watch.
The* MURDERER *and the* LITTLE GIRL *cross the road.
Followed warily by the man in the cap, he joins another
beggar who takes over from him. Dissolve to the* MUR-
DERER *and the* LITTLE GIRL *passing in front of a cheap*

68

café. The two beggars are still following. One of them taps on the window of the café. Immediately a man comes out and takes over trailing the MURDERER.

Dissolve to the window display of a toy shop seen from the inside; it is showing dolls, teddy bears and all kinds of toys. There is a lot of traffic in the street. The MURDERER *and the* LITTLE GIRL *stop in front of the window. He talks to her enthusiastically and she eagerly points out a toy to him. (Still on page 13) The* MURDERER *nods his head. Shot of the entrance of the shop from the street. The* MURDERER *is just about to go in, when the* LITTLE GIRL *sees the chalk mark and grabs his sleeve.*

LITTLE GIRL : Uncle.

MURDERER : What is it?

LITTLE GIRL : You're all dirty.

MURDERER : Where?

He looks at himself in a mirror beside the doorway.

LITTLE GIRL : There, on your shoulder.

Close-up of the MURDERER'S *reflection in the mirror. He turns and sees the M reflected. His eyes bulge. (Still on front cover) Close-up of the letter M. Camera cuts to show the* LITTLE GIRL *and the* MURDERER *together.*

LITTLE GIRL : Here, I'll clean it off.

She tries to rub off the letter with her handkerchief. The MURDERER *is still looking at it in the mirror. Suddenly, he is frightened and turns nervously towards the street. Quick shot of a* BEGGAR, *who hides behind a beer-lorry. Camera cuts back to the* MURDERER *and the* LITTLE GIRL.

LITTLE GIRL *astonished* : Whatever's the matter?

MURDERER : Come on . . . let's go.

He takes her hand and is about to leave when a whistle blows. He lets go of the LITTLE GIRL *and runs away. Resume on the* BEGGAR, *looking around, distraught. Then he whistles through his fingers. Shot of a street corner with a street lamp, there is a pawnbroker's shop in the background. The* MURDERER *runs to the corner, where he hears more shrill whistles.*

Desperate, he runs one way and then the other, before

finally escaping down a side street. Pan after him. A man is waiting on a corner. Nervously, the MURDERER *passes him, hesitates a moment, is about to go up to him, but then rushes off again. This man, too, follows him.*

High shot from above of the MURDERER *in an empty street, he is trying to shake off his pursuers. He turns sharp left and crosses the road, but at the far end two beggars appear. The* MURDERER *retraces his steps and stops undecided in front of a covered entrance gate. In the foreground, a pursuer blocks the middle of the street.*

The gateway, a geometrical structure, leads to the inner courtyard of an office block. The MURDERER *goes in and hides behind a buttress. Camera follows and tracks in on his shoulder; the letter M, although smudged, is still visible. Anxiously, he watches the gateway. Shot of a gate on the other side of the courtyard leading to another street. A policeman passes across it. Cut back to the* MURDERER *in his hiding-place; he is pressing back against the wall as the policeman passes in the background.*

Two of the BEGGARS *appear in the gateway which the* MURDERER *came through.*

Cut to the MURDERER, *poking his head out to look at the street.*

Shot of the three BEGGARS, *who take stock of the situation. One of them gives a signal and the two others go out of shot to right and left to circle the building. The siren of a fire engine is heard in the distance. From the street we see the gateway where the* MURDERER, *a tiny figure, hides behind a pillar. Two fire engines roar past, sirens blaring and lights flashing. When they have gone by, the* FIRST BEGGAR *quickly crosses the road and goes through the arch. The* MURDERER *has disappeared. The two other* BEGGARS *return. Shot of the three* BEGGARS.

2ND BEGGAR : Anyway, he hasn't come out. We would have seen him.

3RD BEGGAR : Impossible.

1ST BEGGAR : He must be in the courtyard, then. He didn't

come out this way either.

2ND BEGGAR : He must be somewhere.

1ST BEGGAR *off* : Perhaps he's gone to hide inside the building.

Pan along the face of the building. A clock strikes six o'clock.

2ND BEGGAR : Hell. The offices will be closing.

1ST BEGGAR : As long as he doesn't get out with all the people coming out.

The 2ND BEGGAR rushes off to the other gateway.

2ND BEGGAR *coming back* : Hell! Here come the first ones already.

1ST BEGGAR : Let's go out into the street.

He disappears. A woman comes out of the building.

1ST BEGGAR : Keep a sharp look out.

The other two run towards the other entrance as the office workers start streaming out, some pushing bicycles. The 2ND BEGGAR, pretending to sell matches, watches them carefully.

VARIOUS VOICES : Excuse me, I just want to light my cigarette . . . My holidays start tomorrow . . . First I'm going to Königsberg . . . With my ulcer, I can't eat things like that . . . The boss came and saw me today.

In the foreground, a car passes, hooting.

Cut to LOHMANN'S ASSISTANT, who is sitting on the windowsill of the MURDERER'S room. Two other plainclothes men are in the foreground.

ASSISTANT : Put out the light, otherwise he'll suspect something when he gets back.

With the light off, the ASSISTANT looks out of the window.

PLAIN-CLOTHES MAN : What's the time?

ASSISTANT : Nearly six-thirty.

A uniformed watchman finishes closing the imposing grille that goes right across the entrance to the office. He greets a passing policeman and goes back into the building.

Medium close-up of the 1ST BEGGAR in a telephone kiosk; he is talking to the underworld bosses.

1st Beggar: He must still be in the building. Anyway, he didn't come out with the others.

The Safe-Breaker, *a cigarette-holder in his mouth, is on the telephone in the crooks' headquarters. Standing beside him,* Schranker, *still wearing overcoat and bowler, plays with his stick.*

Safe-Breaker: Okay . . . yes . . . yes . . . no, just a moment. *He covers the mouthpiece with his hand and talks to* Schranker. The beggars have gone for reinforcements to search the whole area. They say the murderer must still be in the building.

Schranker: Hmm . . . What sort of place is it?

Safe-Breaker *into the telephone*: What sort of building is it?

Beggar *in the kiosk*: Nothing but offices. I don't know what's in the cellar. There's a branch of the Savings Bank on the ground floor, and from the first to the fifth, nothing but offices, and above that lofts.

Over bannisters, the camera frames the half-open door of the loft on the top floor of the office building. On the right of the door is the Night Watchman's *time clock. The* Watchman *comes up and stops astonished in front of the door.*

Watchman *to himself*: Look at that. It's not possible.

He pushes open the door and looks into the loft, camera tracking in on him.

Watchman *shouting*: Anyone there? *He turns on the light.* Hello! Hello! Hello!

Shot of the inside of one of the compartments in the loft. In the foreground, there is a jumble of old furniture and bric-a-brac. The loft area is cut off from the passage by fence-like partitions. The Watchman *passes behind them, camera tracking with him past several compartments.*

Watchman: Anyone there?

He checks one of the doors by shaking it to see whether it is firmly closed. He goes to the next one, where he does the same. Pan across to one of the compartments. In the gloom of the attic we can just make out the Murderer,

72

hiding in a corner. We hear the disappearing footsteps of the WATCHMAN *and the rattle of doors.*

WATCHMAN *off*: Whatever next! *Shouting again.* Anyone there?

Camera cuts to the WATCHMAN *seen through the fence-like partitions. He shakes a door, looks once more along the corridor, then turns away.*

WATCHMAN: Bah! Damn carelessness . . . All that trouble for one door.

He goes out, and camera goes with him. The light goes out. Resume on the MURDERER, *who stands up, tremendously relieved.*

We hear the door out onto the landing close and a key turn in the lock. The MURDERER *stands alert, breathing heavily.*

Long shot of the crooks' room: SCHRANKER, *the* PICK-POCKET, *the* CON-MAN, *the* BURGLAR *and the* SAFE-BREAKER *are grouped around the table.* SCHRANKER, *standing, looks down superciliously, holding his cane handle down on the table. The* SAFE-BREAKER *is on the telephone.*

SAFE-BREAKER *into the telephone*: Yes . . . ah. Good. *He puts down the receiver and turns to the others.* It looks as if the guy is really cornered now. I think we'd better tell the police straight away.

CON-MAN: I agree.

The BURGLAR *and the* PICK-POCKET *also agree.*

SAFE-BREAKER *picking up the telephone again*: Now then, listen carefully . . .

SCHRANKER *violently grabs the receiver from him.*

SCHRANKER *into telephone*: Hello. Just a moment . . . What . . . Okay . . . and ring straight back. *He hangs up.*

Medium close-up of SCHRANKER *between the* BURGLAR *and the* SAFE-BREAKER.

SAFE-BREAKER: What is it? What's got into you?

SCHRANKER *grimly*: Are you mad or something?

SAFE-BREAKER: Why?

SCHRANKER: The police? No . . . we're going to get the guy ourselves . . . Listen . . . now, the time is . . .

73

*There is a slight pause as each man is waiting for some-
one else to make the first move. Clumsily, the* Con-Man
*fumbles for his watch. Group shot of them all round the
table.*

Con-Man : Eight o'clock.

Schranker *in medium close-up* : Good . . . Then, at . . .
nine . . . ten . . . eleven o'clock !

*Camera cuts to the gateway of the office block. From
the street outside we can see through the sliding gates
across the courtyard to the* Watchmen's *office which
is lit up. Somewhere a clock strikes eleven, as a uniformed policeman walks up to the gates and stops. He
rings the bell. One of the watchmen comes out into the
courtyard. Camera cuts to his point-of-view and shows
the empty street through the gates and the policeman
saluting behind them.*

Policeman, *voice of* Schranker: Good evening. Did you
know your gates . . . *Big close-up of the lock* . . . weren't
closed?

Watchman *off* : What? But that's impossible !

*He comes forward, but only his hands holding a lamp
are visible.*

Watchman *off* : I've only just . . . *Close-up of his hand
shaking the grille* . . . But it is . . .

*He stops suddenly. The camera pans to his shocked
face. A sudden cut shows the* Policeman's *gloved hand
pointing a revolver through the ironwork.*

Policeman *off* : Open up and no noise !

Close-up of the Watchman *behind the grille. Reverse
shot of the* Policeman *who turns out to be* Schranker
*in disguise. He is pointing two revolvers. (Still on page
44)*

Schranker : Are you going to open up, then?

Camera cuts to a medium shot from the street.
Schranker *is on the right, his body partly obscuring
the* Watchman *from view.*

Schranker *brutally* : Come on . . . get on with it !

The Watchman *slides back the grille.* Schranker *goes
through and with the barrel of one of his guns pushes*

74

the WATCHMAN *towards his office. The grille stays open.*
SCHRANKER : Get a move on !
Medium close-up of a key ring swaying from the key in the lock of the grille. SCHRANKER *whistles a few bars of the song, '* Be faithful and honest.*'*
Shot of the grille which has been pushed open just wide enough to let one person through at a time. Someone else echoes his whistling. The SAFE-BREAKER *appears in the street and signals to a group of colleagues to follow him. They pass, loaded with bags and suitcases. They all gather in front of the* WATCHMEN'S *office. Camera tilts down slightly over the heads of the whole group. Through the glass partition and half-open door, we see the* WATCHMAN *sitting terrified on a chair with* SCHRANKER *and the* CON-MAN *standing over him.*
SCHRANKER : How many watchmen are there in the building?
The WATCHMAN *does not move.* Okay then, so you don't want to answer, eh?
The WATCHMAN *shakes his head. The* CON-MAN *grabs him by the waistcoat.*
SCHRANKER *ironically* : Okay, then. Okay.
He shuts the door from the inside. Through the glass panes of the door, he can be seen saying something to the WATCHMAN *who still refuses to reply. At a sign from* SCHRANKER, *the* CON-MAN *pulls back the* WATCHMAN'S *arms and ties them behind the back of the chair. After a second's silence, there is a sharp scream.* SCHRANKER *opens the door and speaks to the crooks standing outside.*
SCHRANKER : There are two other watchmen on their rounds.
Camera cuts to a corridor inside the building. One of the other watchmen comes through and resets a time switch on the wall, and then carries on out of sight.
Cut to the attic where the MURDERER *can be seen through the slatted partitions trying to force the lock of the main attic door with his knife. He swears in a low voice.*
MURDERER : Bloody hell !
Close-up of the lock over the MURDERER'S *shoulder. He has removed one of the screws round the lock, but it*

75

does not make any difference.

MURDERER *rattling the lock furiously* : Damn it!

He examines the lock from underneath. On his back the letter M is still visible. In huge close-up, he slips the blade of his knife between the lock and the door, trying to prize open the catch, but the blade snaps and the point falls to the ground. Camera cuts to show the MURDERER *half-standing, half-leaning on the door.*

MURDERER : Damn it!

He raises his arm to throw the knife away.

MURDERER *muttering* : Hell!

He freezes abruptly, arm up and eyes rolling wildly. On the other side of the door, we see a WATCHMAN *passing. He resets a time-switch and prepares to leave. Slight tilt up over the bannisters of the main staircase, the camera frames a door on the fourth floor. Two crooks are working on the lock; one makes an impression, the other passes him the appropriate skeleton key. A third man comes up the stairs. Slight tilt down on the stairs towards the entrance hall.* SCHRANKER *is standing on the bottom steps. Two crooks pass him carrying suitcases.*

SCHRANKER : Careful with the lights. And don't walk like elephants.

The PICK-POCKET *arrives wearing a raincoat and cap.*

SCHRANKER : What's up?

PICK-POCKET : He isn't in the basement. We've been through it with a fine comb and found nothing.

SCHRANKER : Hmm!

PICK-POCKET : Fried and Auguste are still going through the boiler rooms.

The PICK-POCKET *is going on up the stairs when* SCHRANKER *calls him back.*

SCHRANKER : Wait.

Two crooks carrying an unconscious watchman pass them on the stairs.

CROOK *to* SCHRANKER : That's the last one.

SCHRANKER *to* PICK-POCKET : Go up and join Emile. He needs help.

PICK-POCKET : Okay.

76

SCHRANKER : Go on, get a move on!

The PICK-POCKET *hurries up the stairs.*

In the WATCHMEN'S *office, the* SAFE-BREAKER *is poring over a plan on the table. He is dressed rather incongruously in a smart overcoat, silk scarf, and bowler. There is another time-switch on the wall behind him. Propped up against the desk, the second watchman is lying bound and unconscious. The two men carry the third watchman in, followed by the* PICK-POCKET.

PICK-POCKET : Schränker sent me.

SAFE-BREAKER : Good. Listen carefully.

He points to a time-switch, which is then shown in close-up.

Cut to SAFE-BREAKER'S *gloved hand as it comes into frame pointing at the alarm with his cigarette holder.*

SAFE-BREAKER *off* : It's a new type of time-switch.

The gloved hand points to a plan of the building.

SAFE-BREAKER *off* : Here is a general plan of the lay-out. If the time-switches are not reset at exactly the right time, they automatically set off an alarm at the nearest police station. Get it?

Cut to a shot of the time clock.

PICK-POCKET *off* : Sure.

The SAFE-BREAKER'S *hand puts a key into the lock and turns it.*

SAFE-BREAKER *off* : Like that.

The two of them stand in front of the switch. The PICK-POCKET *looks at the plan.*

SAFE-BREAKER : Have you got it?

PICK-POCKET : What do you think I am, some kind of nit?

SAFE-BREAKER : Could be!

He hands him the key. The PICK-POCKET *sets off at a run to make his rounds.*

Camera cuts to SCHRANKER, *who is standing on the staircase, listening to the report of two more of his men.*

1ST CROOK : He isn't in the boiler room either.

SCHRANKER : Fine.

Two men pass with cylinders of gas and an oxy-acetylene cutter.

77

2ND CROOK : We moved all the coal.

SCHRANKER *shouting up to an upper storey* : Hey!

> *Slight tilt up onto the upper landing, the* BURGLAR *is setting up the acetylene cutter in front of a door.*

SCHRANKER : Are you mad?

> *The* BURGLAR *stops his work and straightens up. Camera tilts down from the top of the stairs to show* SCHRANKER *and the other two men looking up.*

SCHRANKER : What if that door's wired up already? Do you want to get the police round here right away?

BURGLAR : Okay. But we've got to get in if we're going to search the whole building.

SCHRANKER *exasperated* : But not by the door, you fool! *He taps his temple.* The office on the floor above . . . go through the ceiling.

> *Shot from above of three crooks coming out of a corridor onto the fourth floor landing. Pan with them as they move towards the bannisters. One of them wearing a beret pulled down over his ears leans over and shouts.*

CROOK : Nothing!

> *Camera cuts to the* BURGLAR *again, now in an office on the second floor. He is drilling with some difficulty through the floor with a power-drill. The* SAFE-BREAKER'S *legs can be seen next to him where he is standing holding a torch. The* BURGLAR'S *tool bag lies open on the floor beside him. (Still on page 61)*
>
> *Cut to the* MURDERER *in medium close-up, who is now seen trying to lever a nail out of one of the wooden uprights on the partition. The broken blade is seen in close-up and then camera tracks back as he struggles to remove the nail by hand. In close-up again, the blade levers the nail out.*
>
> *Cut back to the* BURGLAR *and the* SAFE-BREAKER. *They have now managed to make a decent-sized hole in the floor. Slight tilt down it.* BURGLAR *throws down a rope ladder.*

BURGLAR : Right . . . let's go.

> *He lowers himself through the hole. The* SAFE-BREAKER *leans over and watches him climb down.*

78

The Pick-Pocket, *still studying the plan of the building, has now reached the time-switch outside the main door to the attics. He is just about to put the key in the lock when there is a faint sound of knocking. After glancing round furtively he stops to listen.*

Medium close-up of the Murderer *squatting behind the door, hammering a long nail. In very big close-up, we see that he is flattening one end of the nail with the handle of his knife.*

On the other side, the Pick-Pocket *creeps nearer to the door, listening carefully. The knocking continues. Wildly excited, he makes for the stairs; but he suddenly remembers the time-switch and turns back on his heels and quickly resets it. He pauses for a second to listen again, and then rushes downstairs. From a long way below the* Pick-Pocket *is seen, plan in hand, leaping down the stairs four at a time from the sixth floor landing. Still tracing his descent from below, camera shows some men still forcing a door on the fifth floor landing. (Still on page 61) As the* Pick-Pocket *races past, one of them turns round.*

Crook : Hey, what's up?

The Pick-Pocket, *who has not stopped, is now seen from the fourth floor landing.*

Crook *from the fifth floor off* : Hey, can't you answer me? What's happening? Oy Paul, you might tell us.

A man in a beret runs out of a passage, torch in one hand, revolver in the other. He leans over the bannisters to get a better view of the Pick-Pocket.

Crook *in beret* : What's going on?

Pick-Pocket *breathless, off* : I heard someone banging!

Another crook emerges from the passage. Camera tilts down to the third floor landing. The Pick-Pocket *races past.*

Second Crook *off* : What did you say?

Crook *in beret, off* : What's the hurry?

Camera cuts to the Safe-Breaker, *who is leaning over the hole through the floor, shining his torch, to light up the room below. Hearing the shouting, he jumps up.*

79

From a new angle above the third floor landing, he is seen coming out and grabbing at the PICK-POCKET *as he passes.*

PICK-POCKET *shaking free* : I must see Schränker!

From below the second-floor landing, camera pans with the PICK-POCKET *as he hurls himself towards* SCHRANKER, *pointing frantically upwards.*

PICK-POCKET *out of breath* : In the attic . . . he's in the attic. I heard him knocking. *The* SAFE-BREAKER *joins them.* In the attic . . . he's in the attic!

Camera cuts back to show the MURDERER *has succeeded in bending the nail to make a skeleton key. He puts it into the key-hole and feels around with it. (Still on page 62)*

Back outside the attic door, the metallic sound of the nail inside the keyhole can still be heard, as SCHRANKER *and the others creep up on tip-toe. They stop to listen and the men nudge one another expectantly.*

SCHRANKER : Shhhhhh . . . keep quiet!

The noise of the hammering can be heard clearly.

Close-up of the MURDERER, *crouched behind the door, hammering at the nail. On the floor, he studies his skeleton key.*

MURDERER, *proud of his workmanship* : There!

He turns back to the door and is about to push the key into the keyhole when the handle moves very slightly. The MURDERER *backs away and presses himself against the wall, eyes bulging with terror and staring fixedly at the doorhandle.*

Close-up of the lock from the outside. Two hands are testing a skeleton key selected from an assorted bunch on a large key ring.

Camera cuts back to the attic passageway, facing the door. The MURDERER *presses his ear against the door to listen and then slips off down the passage towards camera. (Still on page 62) Halfway down, he turns back to switch off the light, plunging the place into darkness except for the light filtering in round the edges of the door. His shadow passes in front of the camera and dis-*

80

appears into the recesses of the attic. A moment later, the door is flung open and SCHRANKER *appears in silhouette against the light. Behind him three torches flash on.*

SCHRANKER : Get on with it, then.

Torch beams pass across the wooden partitions.

SCHRANKER *off* : He must be there.

OTHER VOICES *off* : There's the switch.

Camera cuts to the passage seen from the door. The lights come on. The passage is now seen as it goes through the partition of a compartment, piled up with old furniture.

SCHRANKER *off* : Force the locks.

Some men pass down the passage.

VOICES : Come on. Hurry up! Get a move on!

Camera tracks back slightly and pans onto the door of the compartment. Then it tracks in again.

VOICES : Come on. Off with it.

Two crooks force the door.

Back in the WATCHMEN'S *office, the* CON-MAN *is seated by the window. The* PICK-POCKET *comes in.*

PICK-POCKET : We've got him.

CON-MAN *getting up* : What?

PICK-POCKET : He's in the attic.

CON-MAN : Is that so?

In medium close-up, the FIRST WATCHMAN *moves. He is still lying tied up on the floor. While the two crooks are talking, he makes an effort to haul himself onto his knees and reach the alarm.*

PICK-POCKET *off* : Yes, I heard someone hammering . . .

CON-MAN *off* : Who?

PICK-POCKET *off* : . . . and immediately told Schränker . . .

CON-MAN *off* : What did he say?

PICK-POCKET *off* : He's already up there with eight men.

CON-MAN *off* : Oh, great!

PICK-POCKET *off* : They'll get him any moment.

CON-MAN *off* : You think so?

Camera cuts back to the two crooks face to face.

PICK-POCKET : I just came down to tell you.

CON-MAN : Great.

Pick-Pocket *importantly*: If I hadn't been on the alert we might have been looking for him for hours.

The Con-Man *rises quickly and grabs the* Pick-Pocket *by the shoulder. We see the* Watchman *on his knees, his handcuffed hands lifted towards the alarm bell.*

Con-Man *off*: Look out . . . the watchman!

Large close-up of the Watchman's *hands as they snatch awkwardly at the alarm which is connected directly to the local police station. A bell rings as the camera cuts to a ticker-tape machine in the station which starts to operate by unrolling a punched tape. A* Policeman *comes into shot and leans over to read the tape.*

Policeman: Three . . . one . . . four.

Close-up of the machine with the punched tape emerging.

Policeman *off*: Three, one, four.

Close-up of a filing cabinet. A hand flicks through some cards and takes one out.

Another Policeman: Three, one, four.

Cut back to the attic passageway; the Pick-Pocket *bursts through to warn the men searching there. He shouts something incomprehensible.*

A Crook: Are you crazy? *General hubbub.*

Pick-Pocket: Yes, the cops'll be here any minute. The watchman gave the alarm.

Crook: Let's get out of here! *They make for the door.*

Schranker *off*: Stop! Quiet! *He comes into shot.* We've five minutes more and six more compartments to search. Carry on. Get on with it. Only hurry! Come on, now!

The Crooks *start work again. One of them fiddles with the lock on a door.* Schranker *pushes him aside.*

Schranker: Out of the way. You can't do it like that.

He crashes against the door with all his weight to break it open. Camera cuts to the Murderer *hidden in one of the compartments, weak with fear. Light feebly penetrates a skylight. The sound of doors being forced open comes gradually closer.*

Voice: He's not in here.

Schranker *off*: Next door!

Noise of splintering wood and tearing hinges.

SCHRANKER *off* : Come on. Quicker.

The noise draws nearer and the MURDERER *ducks down further and further into his corner.*

VOICE : Not here either.

SCHRANKER *off* : Come on. Keep it up ! Next door.

As we hear the noise of another breaking door, the MURDERER *disappears completely behind the bric-a-brac. Only his hat is visible.*

SCHRANKER *off* : Quick. We've only three minutes left.

VOICE : Hurry up. Quickly !

SEVERAL VOICES : This one hasn't got a padlock . . . he must be here . . . go on, open it . . . it's locked from the inside . . . let *me* do it !

SCHRANKER *off* : Hurry up. Only one minute left !

The noise is deafening as the door is forced down and furniture crashes to the floor. Panic-stricken, the MURDERER *leaps to his feet, spot-lit by a powerful torch beam. His face is grotesquely twisted with fear. Backing away, he stumbles against a grandfather clock. (Still on page 63)*

VOICE : Here he is . . . here he is . . . the bastard !

Back in the courtyard, we see a parked car in the street behind the gates which are still pulled back. The SAFE-BREAKER *is on guard by the opening and he checks on the men as they stream silently through, loaded with equipment, which they throw into the car before slipping out of sight down the street.*

SAFE-BREAKER : Get going. Hurry up ! *He whistles through his fingers.* Everybody out !

The CON-MAN *runs past, pulling his overcoat on over a* WATCHMAN'S *jacket. The* SAFE-BREAKER *pushes him outside.*

SAFE-BREAKER : Go on. Move ! *Other crooks pass through.* Come on, hurry up. Quick !

The CON-MAN *goes back inside.*

CON-MAN : Christ ! Get out while you can, you fool !

The CON-MAN *makes for the door as the* SAFE-BREAKER *runs past the* WATCHMEN'S *office. Camera follows a few stragglers coming out of the building.*

SAFE-BREAKER : Anybody left ?

CROOK : A few up top . . . they're on their way.

SAFE-BREAKER : No reason for you to wait for them. With or without the guy, it doesn't matter, get away. *He throws up his arms in despair.* What are they up to, for Christ's sake . . . Bloody hell. *He goes back into the building.* At last. Thank God!

A final group leaves the building and the SAFE-BREAKER *follows them. Camera tilts up slightly as two men carry the* MURDERER *down the steps, tied up and struggling inside a rolled carpet.* SCHRANKER, *still in his policeman's uniform, dominates the scene as he stands behind them supervising the operation. (Still on page 64) He and the* SAFE-BREAKER *are the last to leave. The courtyard and the street beyond are left quiet and deserted. There is an ominous silence. Slight tilt from above of the* WATCH-MEN'S *office where the* FIRST WATCHMAN *lies unconscious, wrists handcuffed together, and then pan across to the two other watchmen who are slumped together in a corner, tied up and unconscious. (Still on page 81)*

Shot from high above down the hole cut through the ceiling from the second floor. A torch beam sweeps across the floor of the room below and rises towards the opening.

BURGLAR *off* : Hey! He's not down here. *No reply.* Oh! Who's pulled up the ladder? *The* BURGLAR'S *face comes into view looking up from below, and repeats:* Who's pulled up the ladder? *Someone throws the ladder down into the hole. Irritably:* Bunch of morons.

As his head and shoulders emerge from the opening, a torch clicks on and shines straight into his face.

BURGLAR : Hello.

A second torch lights him up.

A VOICE : Hands up.

BURGLAR *curtly* : How can I put my hands up when I'm trying to hang onto the ladder, eh?

THE VOICE : Out of there.

Camera tracks up and back. The BURGLAR *climbs out of the hole, sits on the edge and raises his hands. Camera tracks further back. He is surrounded by policemen.*

BURGLAR *jokingly* : For once I'm innocent . . .

The voice continues over as camera cuts to INSPECTOR
GROEBER'S *office.*

BURGLAR : . . . as a new born babe.

The BURGLAR *is sitting by* GROEBER'S *desk. A lamp shines
into his face. Camera frames them both in profile.*
GROEBER *is a distinguished, well-groomed man of about
fifty. Behind them sits a secretary, a little old man who
looks from one to the other over the top of his spectacles.*
GROEBER *cuts a cigar and from behind the lamp leans
towards the* BURGLAR.

GROEBER : This will surprise you, Franz, but I believe you.

BURGLAR *in reverse angle, not altogether reassured* : Hmmm.
Ha, ha. *He laughs nervously.* Then everything is in order,
Inspector. *He gets up.* I can leave then . . .

GROEBER'S *hand comes into shot and gestures to him to
sit down.*

GROEBER *off* : One minute !

GROEBER *is now seen facing the camera. He picks up a
packet of cigarettes. Resume on the* BURGLAR *who is
now standing.* GROEBER'S *hand comes into shot holding
the cigarettes.*

GROEBER *off* : Cigarette ?

BURGLAR : Oh, boy.

*Crestfallen, he slumps back into his chair and takes a
cigarette.*

GROEBER : I'll take your word for it. *He leans back, rocking
his chair.* On condition you tell me . . .

He pauses. The BURGLAR *waits, holding an unlit cigarette in one hand and a burning match in the other.
Camera intercuts between the two men.*

GROEBER : . . . who the man was you were looking for . . .
and found in the building.

*On these last words, he lets himself fall forward, while
the* BURGLAR *puts out the match and lays the cigarette
on the table. He feigns surprise.*

BURGLAR : I don't understand, Inspector. A man, you said.
No, I don't know anything about that, Inspector. There must
be some mistake. I don't know anything.

GROEBER *and the* BURGLAR *are shown in profile, with*

the SECRETARY *behind them at the end of the table,
facing the camera.*

BURGLAR: Nothing at all.

GROEBER: Of course. *Slyly.* Only I don't understand why you
are covering up for the gang who left you in the lurch. *He
relights his cigar.* Funny friends! Leaving you right in it and
running off. Bah!

BURGLAR *smiling maliciously*: That won't wash with me,
Inspector. GROEBER *takes some notes. The* SECRETARY *takes
the opportunity to sharpen some pencils. The* BURGLAR *looks
round him worriedly. He tries to read what* GROEBER *is
writing, but cannot make it out.*

BURGLAR: After all . . . *Not very sure of himself, he pauses;
then, after a moment, he begins again* . . . After all I'm not
risking very much.

Close-up of the hole in the floor.

BURGLAR *off*: Maybe a little bit of damage. But nothing was
stolen.

Camera cuts back to GROEBER *in medium close-up.*

GROEBER: Of course, something was stolen. In fact a good
deal . . .

The BURGLAR *leans forward, surprised.*

BURGLAR: What? *He is rising to the bait.* Stolen? How much?

GROEBER: If you talk I'll tell you.

BURGLAR: I've already told you. I don't know anything.

GROEBER: All right. *He gets up.* Well, think about it. It's
amazing what one remembers . . . *turning on the ceiling
light* . . . when one's left alone for an hour or two. *We hear
the door opening.* Take him away!

A hand is placed on the BURGLAR'S *shoulder and he rises
and leaves the room. Camera tracks in on* GROEBER, *who
watches him go thoughtfully.*

GROEBER *to the* SECRETARY: Get the night watchman sent in.
He sits down and opens a dossier.

SECRETARY *off*: Get the night watchman, Damowitz.

GROEBER *raises his eyes and looks towards the door.
Camera follows his look. The* SECRETARY *shows the*
WATCHMAN *in.*

GROEBER *off*: Sit down.

90

The WATCHMAN *sits in the armchair in front of the desk.*
Pan to GROEBER, *who continues to study the dossier.*

GROEBER: Now then, you said in your statement . . . *He raises his eyes to the* WATCHMAN. Listen carefully.

The SECRETARY'S *hand turns off the light on the desk and picks up a pencil.*

GROEBER: You may have to repeat it under oath. *He reads from the dossier.* That you clearly heard . . .

The WATCHMAN *is seen in medium close-up, his right cheek swollen.*

GROEBER *off*: . . . that one of the burglars said to another, ' We've found him . . .'

The WATCHMAN *nods his head, winces with pain and holds his cheek.*

GROEBER *off*: '. . . I've discovered the bloke. He is in the attic.' Is that correct?

WATCHMAN: Yes, Inspector . . . ooooh. *He grimaces with pain.* Yes, Inspector . . . I'll swear to that whenever you wish.

Reverse shot of GROEBER, *who closes the dossier.*

GROEBER: Right. You may go home and rest now. But please keep yourself at the disposal of the police.

The WATCHMAN *gets up.*

WATCHMAN: Of course, Inspector . . . oooh. *Painfully.* Good day, Inspector.

He goes out, holding his jaw askew.

GROEBER: Good day.

He remains for a moment, deep in thought. Then camera tracks in as he picks up the telephone.

GROEBER *on the telephone*: Tell me, is Inspector Lohmann in the building? . . . Oh, good . . . He's talking to somebody? No, it doesn't matter. I'll come up.

Camera cuts to show LOHMANN *sitting at his desk smoking a cigar; he is framed against the large map of the city on the wall behind him. Now he is in shirt-sleeves, his collar open and tie loosened, and he looks tired and harassed. He is on the telephone, and with one hand pours out coffee from an enamel coffee pot.*

LOHMANN *on the telephone*: What? Good. Hasn't come in yet . . . You're watching the old girl, that Mrs. Winkler, eh?

91

There is a knock on the door.

LOHMANN : Come in.

Shot from below under the desk at floor level, we see that LOHMANN *is stretched out in his chair, lying rather than sitting. (Still on page 82) From this angle, the size of his stomach is enormously exaggerated and we can see that his trousers are unbuttoned at the waist; chewing at his cigar, he hangs up.*

LOHMANN : Hell!

Camera cuts back to show LOHMANN *behind his desk, and it pans slightly to pick up* GROEBER *who has just come in, a dossier under his arm. He sits on the edge of the desk.* LOHMANN *adds some milk to his coffee from a carton.*

LOHMANN : What do you want?

GROEBER : I wanted to ask you . . .

Camera tracks in to isolate LOHMANN *who drinks his coffee.*

GROEBER *off* : . . . a favour.

LOHMANN *in close-up, drinking* : Ugh . . . what muck.

GROEBER *off* : I wanted to ask you . . .

Camera tracks back as GROEBER'S *hand places the dossier on the table.*

GROEBER *off* : Anyway, read a bit of that.

LOHMANN *takes a bite from a biscuit and picks up the dossier.*

Close-up of LOHMANN'S *hand holding the dossier marked ' REPORTS.'*

LOHMANN *off* : Reports?

GROEBER *off* : Yes.

The hand opens the dossier. The first typewritten sheet carries the date 25th November, 1930.

GROEBER *off* : Burglary in an office block.

The page is turned.

Dissolve to a shot of the ticker-tape machine and the punched tape.

Dissolve to a general view of the office building at Benna-strasse 29-33 and Ostend-allee 114-117.

LOHMANN *off* : Bennastrasse?

Dissolve to the main entrance of the building with gates half-open and the WATCHMEN'S *office illuminated.*

LOHMANN *off* : That's a very quiet neighbourhood.

Dissolve to the WATCHMAN *unconscious on the floor of his office.*

LOHMANN *off* : . . . Perhaps it's not as quiet as all that . . .

Dissolve to the office again where the other bound watchmen are seen in the corner.

LOHMANN *off* : Hell, this is becoming serious.

Dissolve to an open door on the landing with the lock cut.

Dissolve to another door, also forced.

Dissolve back to a close-up of another page of the dossier. It is turned.

Dissolve to another door. A drill is still sticking in a hole and all round the lock there is a circle of holes.

LOHMANN *off* : Did they intend to empty the whole place, then?

Dissolve to the basement of the building where the door to the coal-hole has been forced.

LOHMANN *amazed, off* : What can they have been looking for in the coal?

Dissolve to the boiler room, seen through a shattered door.

LOHMANN *off* : Look at that. It's incredible.

Dissolve to another page of the dossier as it is turned.

Dissolve to the corridor of the attic. The door of every compartment has been forced.

LOHMANN *off* : Good Lord.

Dissolve to the rear of the attic. The last few doors are completely smashed to pieces.

LOHMANN *off, clicking his tongue* : This is madness!

Dissolve to the last compartment showing all the furniture turned upside down.

Dissolve to a close-up of the hole in the ceiling on the second floor, with the rope ladder and the abandoned drill.

LOHMANN *off* : Ah, now it makes sense. They were after the safe.

Dissolve to a close-up of an old safe. It has not been touched.

LOHMANN *off*: Good God. What's that all about?

Dissolve to a close-up of another safe, also unharmed.

LOHMANN *off*: I don't understand it at all.

Close-up of another safe, also intact.

LOHMANN *off*: They haven't even attacked that one. Were they all crazy or something?

Dissolve to a quick shot of a page of the dossier turning. Then camera cuts to show the two of them in the office.

LOHMANN *lifting his head*: Well, I'll be damned!

GROEBER: Well, what have you got to say? Nothing stolen, but a man was taken away. God knows where.

LOHMANN: Fantastic!

He puts his cigar-holder down on a plate and prepares another cigar.

GROEBER: And Franz — the burglar we arrested — isn't talking. Frightened evidently. Actually I know him well . . . he is one of those burglars who would rather jump from the fifth floor than get mixed up in a murder.

LOHMANN *finishes cutting his cigar and starts to suck it.*

GROEBER: If we could . . . set a trap for him? *A huge smile spreads across* LOHMANN'S *face.* Could you help me out, Lohmann?

LOHMANN *raising his cigar*: I see what you are getting at . . . well then, let's take a look at this Franz.

Camera cuts to a prison cell where the BURGLAR *is stretched out on a bed, his legs in the foreground. A* DETECTIVE *comes in.*

DETECTIVE: For questioning.

The scene fades to black.

Back in LOHMANN'S *office, the* BURGLAR *is seen examining a plaque on the wall. The* DETECTIVE *who brought him in stands in the background.*

Close-up of the plaque. It is a list of the members of the Murder Squad, with names, addresses and telephone numbers. Under 'Head of Department' we can read: 'Karl Lohmann,' followed by an address and telephone number. Camera cuts back to show the BURGLAR'S *back view as he stares at the list.*

BURGLAR *unhappily* : Inspector Karl Lohmann . . .

A door opens. The BURGLAR *turns.* LOHMANN *has come in, hands in pockets, sucking a cigar. The* BURGLAR *moves towards him.*

BURGLAR *frightened* : What do you want with me? *Shouting.* What does the Murder Squad want with me?

After a moment, LOHMANN *comes into shot. He stops in front of the* BURGLAR.

LOHMANN : Yes, old boy . . . Your case has been passed over to me now.

The BURGLAR, *very worried, wrings his hands.* LOHMANN *stands in front of him, in profile.*

BURGLAR : But . . . but why? Whatever for?

LOHMANN : You did your work a little too well.

The BURGLAR *nervously unbuttons his collar.*

BURGLAR *in a choked voice* : Yes?

LOHMANN *meaningfully* : One of the watchmen . . .

Camera cuts to DAMOWITZ, *the* WATCHMAN, *sitting at a table, in his home, an enormous plate of sausage and cabbage in front of him. He drinks some beer, wipes his moustache and digs into another sausage.*

Camera cuts back to LOHMANN *and the* BURGLAR.

BURGLAR *in a choked voice* : Dead?

LOHMANN *paces round his office; camera pans with him.*

LOHMANN : Planning and assisting with a murder . . . It's a bad show, Franz.

BURGLAR *off, still choking over his words* : I can't go on with it. I don't want to have anything to do with that.

We see both of them as LOHMANN *picks up a dossier and flicks through it.*

BURGLAR *breaking down* : I'll tell you everything . . . everything I know.

LOHMANN *off-hand* : Very wise, but unfortunately too late.

The BURGLAR *moves nearer and can be seen pleading with* LOHMANN *who turns his back on him.*

BURGLAR : Inspector, it *can't* be too late . . . please, Inspector . . . But, it isn't possible. Listen, I'm going to tell you everything . . . everything. Even who we were looking for in that damn building.

LOHMANN *straightens up, triumphant and interested, but does not turn round.*

LOHMANN : Well, then.

BURGLAR : The murderer . . . the child murderer.

Medium close-up of LOHMANN *as his mouth drops open in amazement, and his cigar falls out onto the table. There is a pause.* LOHMANN *is dumbfounded and without thinking he raises a shaky hand to remove the cigar from his lips. He looks confused for a moment, but quickly recovering his composure, he picks it up from the dossier where it had fallen.*

LOHMANN *with dawning realisation* : What? What? . . . Who?

BURGLAR *distraught* : The child murderer, Inspector.

LOHMANN *puffs out a great cloud of cigar smoke which completely obscures his face. He strides across the room flapping a hand to disperse the smoke-screen around him.*

LOHMANN : Wait.

Very quick pan with him towards a door which he closes behind him.

In the toilet LOHMANN, *seen from above, leans against the basin and puts his head under the cold tap.*

Camera cuts back to the office in medium shot, where the BURGLAR *waits in total despair.*

BURGLAR *sighing* : This had to happen to me! Of all people. *A door opens behind him. He turns.* LOHMANN *comes back in, looking happy and satisfied. He has his jacket on and, rubbing his hands, sits down behind his desk. Camera pans with him and then tracks back to frame him and the* BURGLAR. *After a while,* LOHMANN *takes out a cigar and cuts it, with a pair of scissors.*

LOHMANN : Right . . . Now, we're going to have a little talk.

BURGLAR *hopelessly* : If you want to, Inspector. (*Still on page 82*).

LOHMANN : And mind you don't lie. *He pauses.* Okay, let's start. What have you got to do with the murderer and where have you taken him?

BURGLAR : Well now, Inspector, you know the old . . .

Cut to the battered façade of an empty factory, almost

96

a ruin.

BURGLAR *off* : . . . distillery of Kuntz and Levy . . .

Cut to a corner of the building.

LOHMANN *off* : The one that went bankrupt?

In the gloom of an abandoned workshop inside the factory, a staircase can just be made out to the right. Inarticulate cries are heard in the distance, gradually drawing nearer. Two men come down the steps and disappear into the gloom.

MURDERER *off* : What do you want with me? Let me go . . . let me go!

A VOICE *roughly* : Go on . . . keep moving . . . go on.

Shot of the two men reappearing, they are pushing the MURDERER up a short stairway. He is struggling furiously although his jacket has been pulled over his head. At the top of the steps a third man comes to help them. Group shot of them all.

MURDERER *struggling* : I've done nothing to you . . . Let me go, you swine.

From the bottom of another flight of steps, the camera tilts up to an iron door, which is flung open. A foot appears on the top step, but no one appears for a minute as there is obviously a scuffle going on at the top of the stairs. The third man comes down the steps.

MURDERER *off* : Let me go.

The two others push the MURDERER down the steps. He slips on the steps.

MURDERER : Bastards!

The MURDERER has fallen to the bottom of the steps and the two men stand on the platform at the top.

MURDERER : Bunch of bastards!

One of the men closes the door. The MURDERER drags his coat off his head.

MURDERER : What do you want with me? Bastards! What do you want?

He turns round and stops dead in his tracks. (Still on page 83) Camera cuts back to show the huge factory cellar from his point-of-view, where assorted members of the underworld can be seen watching him. Camera pans along the entire length of the cellar to reveal that a vast crowd has assembled — crooks and their wives, tarts, pimps and beggars — most of them standing, with the older members seated on boxes and crates. There is absolute silence and no one moves. Pan continues until it reaches a trestle table set up in front of them. Behind it sit the PICK-POCKET, *the* CON-MAN *and the* SAFE-BREAKER *on either side of* SCHRANKER. (*Still on page 84*) *It is obviously a crude form of tribunal and, as usual,* SCHRANKER *is in charge.*

MURDERER : Help!

Camera cuts back to the MURDERER *and the two men on the stairs.*

MURDERER : Help! Let me go. I want to get out . . . *He tries to climb up a few steps.* I want to get out. Get out.

A general view of the tribunal, lit only by a single bulb hanging from the ceiling.

MURDERER *off* : Let me out!

SCHRANKER *firmly* : You will not get out of here.

The two men on the staircase block the MURDERER'S *way. He turns back to face the crowd.*

MURDERER : But, gentlemen . . . *His hair falling over his face, he comes down the stairs. Camera tracks in on him as he appeals to them.* Please, I don't even know what you want me for. *He takes a few hesitant paces forward.* I beg you. Set me free. There must be some mistake . . . *A hand comes into frame above his head, feeling around in the air. A mist . . .*

The hand falls on the MURDERER'S *shoulder. His voice breaks off with a cry of terror.* (*Still on page 84*)

BLIND BEGGAR *off* : No . . . No . . . No mistake . . . Impossible. There's no mistake.

Camera tracks back to show the MURDERER *and the* BLIND BEGGAR. *The* MURDERER *turns towards him.*

THE BLIND BEGGAR *withdrawing his hand* : No, no mistake.

MURDERER : But . . . what do you mean?

Camera tracks further back so that the BLIND BEGGAR'S *other arm comes into view. He is holding a doll-shaped balloon. He shows it to the* MURDERER.

BLIND BEGGAR : Do you recognise it? It is a balloon like the one you gave to little Elsie Beckmann. (*Still on page 109*)

The MURDERER *stiffens with fear at the mention of that name. The* BLIND BEGGAR *holds the string of the doll-shaped balloon and lets it rise up as far as the string will go. Seen from above, the* MURDERER *follows the balloon's ascent with horrified eyes. It sways gently very close to the camera. The faces of the crowd are a confused blur in the background.*

BLIND BEGGAR *off* : A balloon like that . . .

MURDERER *gibbering* : El . . . El . . . Elsie . . . El . . . Elsie.

He backs away, terrified by the balloon, until he stumbles against the table. The camera follows him.

MURDERER, *his voice becoming more and more high-pitched* : No, no, no . . .

Camera cuts quickly onto the MURDERER'S *back. Behind him, we see the* BLIND BEGGAR *and the staircase guarded by the two men.*

SCHRANKER *off* : Where did you . . .

On SCHRANKER'S *first words, the* MURDERER *turns to face the camera.*

An immediate cut to SCHRANKER *who has a photograph in front of him on the table of a little girl.*

SCHRANKER *leaning forward* : . . . bury little Martha?

Cut back to the MURDERER *who walks forwards towards the camera as the* BLIND BEGGAR *is led away by one of the crooks.*

MURDERER : But . . . but I never . . . I never even knew her.

SCHRANKER *sarcastically* : Oh yes, very good. You didn't even know her. *He waves another photograph.* And what about this one?

Cut back to the MURDERER *who backs away, now help-less with fright. A cutting from a newspaper is shown in medium close-up, lying on the table.*

SCHRANKER *off* : And this one?

Camera cuts to the MURDERER, *who chews at his fingers. Cut back to* SCHRANKER'S *gloved hand showing a third photograph. We recognise* ELSIE'S *face.*

SCHRANKER *off* : . . . and this one, you didn't know this one either, eh?

The MURDERER *is seen now crazy with fright. Panic-stricken, he spins round in a mad dash for the exit. One of the men who brought him in is sitting at the foot of the stairs; he jumps up to bar the way as the crowd begin to jump up and shout hysterically. (Still on page 109)*

VOICES : Stop him . . . Stop him . . . don't let him escape!
From one end of the cellar we see the crowd surging forward. Only SCHRANKER *remains calmly seated.*

VOICES : Stop him . . . he mustn't get away!
Camera cuts back to the MURDERER *who barges past the crook on the stairs, pushing him violently out of the way, and manages to climb towards the door.*

VOICES : Quick, stop him . . . Hold him . . . Look out . . . the door!
We now see the top of the stairs and the door which the MURDERER *tries to open, but a crook grabs him by the collar.*

A VOICE : Hold him . . . hang onto him.
From the same angle but closer, the MURDERER *hangs onto the door handle with both hands. The crook holds him from behind. Two others come to his aid.*

A VOICE : Go on . . . Go on . . . Hit him . . . Belt him!
Close-up of the MURDERER'S *convulsed face. A hand seizes him by the throat. (Still on page 110)*

MURDERER *in a strangled voice* : Let me go . . . Let me go!
Medium shot of the three men trying to make the MURDERER *loosen his grip. A fourth crook comes up the stairs to help them. One of them kicks him on the shins. The general shouting gets louder. Close-up of the crook kicking the* MURDERER, *then cut to a close-up of the* MURDERER'S *hand still grasping the handle.*

A VOICE : Go on . . . on his shins.
Camera cuts quickly to the fighter's legs. The MURDERER *receives another violent kick in the shins. Cut back to a medium shot of the struggle at the door. A crook tries to hit the* MURDERER'S *hands.*

VOICES : Heave . . . ho. Heave . . . ho.

Close-up of the crook's fist violently striking the MUR-
DERER'S *fingers. The shock makes him let go. Camera
cuts back to a medium shot of the group as they draw
back from the* MURDERER *and throw him down the
stairs. The camera pans quickly as he falls. He lands
heavily on the ground, banging his head sharply against
some old timbers lying against the wall. He lies twisting
with pain while the crowd cheers and hoots triumphantly.*

MURDERER *almost in tears*: You have no right to treat me
like this!

VOICES : We'll show you what right we have!

MURDERER *groaning*: You have no right to hold me here.
    *Camera cuts to part of the crowd. A prostitute gets up,
    furiously.*

PROSTITUTE *screaming fanatically* : Right? Someone like you
doesn't have any rights. *Roaring.* Kill him!

A MAN *next to her, rising* : Yes, kill him!

PROSTITUTE : We must put him down like a mad dog!
    There is a general view of the crowd, now very animated.

A VOICE : Crush him.

SCHRANKER *turning impatiently to the crowd* : Quiet!

A VOICE : Kill him! . . . Kill him!

SCHRANKER *shouting* : Shut up!
    *The crowd is calmed by an imperious gesture from
    *SCHRANKER. *When the noise dies down completely, he
    turns towards the* MURDERER.

SCHRANKER : You talk of rights . . . You will get your rights.
*Camera tracks, in close-up, across the attentive faces of the
crowd, as* SCHRANKER *continues off:* We are all law experts
here, from six weeks in Tegel, to fifteen years in Brandenburg.* *Close-up of* SCHRANKER. You will get your rights . . .
you will even have a lawyer. *Ironically.* Everything will be
done according to the rule of the law.
    Camera cuts to the MURDERER *crouching in a corner
    like a toad.*

MURDERER *screaming* : A lawyer? . . . A lawyer? . . . I don't
need a lawyer . . . Who is accusing me? You, maybe? *You?*

---

* Tegel and Brandenburg are two of Berlin's prisons.

A hand taps him on the shoulder. The MURDERER *turns round. Camera pans up, following his glance to frame a fairly old, ill-shaven man, who leans towards him across a wooden barrier. He is a* LAWYER. *In front of him, on a chest, a pile of Criminal and Civil law books.*

LAWYER: Eh . . . just a moment . . . If I were you sir, I'd keep quiet. Your life's at stake . . . in case you didn't know.

The MURDERER *rises and leans towards the* LAWYER *seated behind his chest. He stares at him in amazement.*

MURDERER: Who are you?

LAWYER *greeting him*: I have the dubious honour of being your defence counsel. But I am afraid it won't be much use to you.

The LAWYER *superciliously blows some dust from his notebook.*

MURDERER: But . . . but . . . Do you want to kill me then? *Horrified.* Murder me, just like that?

SCHRANKER *in close-up*: We just want to render you harmless. That's what we want . . . but you'll only be harmless when you're dead.

Camera cuts back to a medium shot of the LAWYER *and the* MURDERER.

MURDERER *begging*: But if you kill me it'll be cold-blooded murder! *Derisive laughter echoes round the cellar. The* LAWYER *sighs and shrugs his shoulders.* I demand that you hand me over to the police. *The laughter increases. He raises his voice.* I demand to be handed over to the jurisdiction of the common law.

This is greeted by loud laughter from the crowd. Camera cuts to SCHRANKER *and the* CON-MAN *unconcerned; behind them, the crowd rocks with laughter.*

A VOICE: Quite a performance . . . That's not bad, that, ha, ha, ha!

SCHRANKER *to the* MURDERER: That would suit you, wouldn't it?

CON-MAN *expostulating*: Anything else you'd like.

SCHRANKER: So that you can invoke paragraph fifty-one.

A VOICE: That's it.

SCHRANKER: . . . And spend the rest of your life in an institution at the state's expense . . . And then you'd escape . . . or else there'd be a pardon and there you are, free as air, with a pass, protected by the law because of mental illness. *Laughter.* Off again chasing little girls. *A pause.* No, no. *Very dry.* We're not going to let that happen.

A VOICE *echoing*: No, no, no.

SCHRANKER: We must make you powerless. You must disappear.

A VOICE: Bravo . . . he must disappear.

Medium close-up of the MURDERER *sobbing with fear.*

MURDERER: But I can't help what I do. *He falls to his knees and miserably hides his face in his hands.* I can't help it . . . I can't . . . I can't . . . I can't help it.

Camera cuts quickly back to show the crowd from one side. In the front row, a crook rises to his feet.

CROOK *with an evil laugh*: The old story.

Camera tilts down slightly over the MURDERER, *who has fallen to his knees. Helplessly, he lowers his hands.*

MURDERER *in complete despair*: What do you know about it? What are you saying? If it comes to that, who are you? What right have you to speak? *He turns his head to look at them all.* Who are you . . . All of you? . . . Criminals! Perhaps you're even proud of yourselves? Proud of being able to break safes, to climb into buildings or cheat at cards . . . Things you could just as well keep your fingers off . . . You wouldn't need to do all that if you had learnt a proper trade . . . or if you worked. If you weren't a bunch of lazy bastards . . . But I . . . *His hands clutch at his chest.* I can't help myself! I haven't any control over this evil thing that's inside me — the fire, the voices, the torment! *(Still on page 110)*

Cut to a slight tilt on SCHRANKER *sitting at the table; behind him part of the crowd.*

Resume on the MURDERER.

MURDERER *agonised*: Always . . . always, there's this evil force inside me . . . It's there all the time, driving me out to wander through the streets . . . following me . . . silently, but I can feel it there . . . It's me, pursuing myself, because . . .

SCHRANKER: You mean to say you *have* to murder?

Medium close-up of an old man in the crowd, nodding

103

thoughtfully, moved by the MURDERER'S *genuine anguish.*

MURDERER *off* : I want to escape . . . to escape from myself! *Camera cuts to two other crooks. One of them seems very moved* . . . but it's impossible. I can't. I can't escape. *Return to the panting* MURDERER. I have to obey it. I have to run . . . run . . . streets . . . endless streets. I want to escape. I want to get away. *Cut to two prostitutes, one of them nervously twisting a handkerchief.* And I am pursued by ghosts. Ghosts of mothers. And of those children . . . They never leave me. *Shouting desperately.* They are there, there, always, always. *In close-up.* Always . . . except . . . *He lowers his voice* . . . except when I do it . . . when I . . . *He raises his hands towards his neck, (Still on page 111) as though he were about to strangle a victim, then he lets them fall limp at his sides.* Then I can't remember anything . . . And afterwards I see those posters and I read what I've done . . . I read . . . and . . . and read . . . Did I do that? But I can't remember anything about it . . . But who will believe me? Who knows what it feels like to be me? How I'm forced to act . . . *His eyes close in ecstasy.* How I must . . . Don't want to, but must . . . *He screams.* Must . . . Don't want to . . . must. And then . . . a voice screams . . . I can't bear to hear it. *He throws himself against the wooden barrier in a paroxysm covering his ears with his hands.*

MURDERER *at the height of his fit* : I can't . . . I can't go on. Can't go on . . . Can't go on . . . Can't go on . . .

    Camera cuts back to SCHRANKER *and the* SAFE-BREAKER; *the crowd behind them.* SCHRANKER *rises to his feet.*

MURDERER *off, his voice dying away* : I can't go on . . .

SCHRANKER : The accused has said that he cannot help himself. That is to say : he has to murder. As this is the case, he has pronounced his own death sentence.

VOICES *off* : Hurrah . . . that's true . . . Hurrah.

SCHRANKER : Someone who admits to being a compulsive murderer should be snuffed out, like a candle.

A VOICE : Hurrah.

SCHRANKER *louder* : This man must be wiped out, eliminated.

    Applause and shouts. Medium close-up of the MURDERER

*on his knees, he rubs his head against the barrier, his
hands still over his ears. The noise continues.*

Cut back to a quick view of SCHRANKER *and the* SAFE-
BREAKER, *the crowd in a frenzy behind them.*

VARIOUS VOICES : Hurrah . . . Perfect, just what I think . . .
Hurrah!

Medium shot of the LAWYER *who gets up. On his right,
the* MURDERER *crouches.*

LAWYER : I wish to speak.

SCHRANKER *off* : The defence lawyer will speak.

LAWYER *ironically* : Our very honourable President . . .

He rubs his hands together. There is a quick shot of
SCHRANKER *who has just sat down.*

LAWYER *off* : . . . who is, I believe, wanted by the police for
three murders . . .

SCHRANKER *very angry* : That's got nothing to do with it!

LAWYER *continuing* : . . . claims that because my client acts
under an irresistible impulse, he is condemned to death.

A VOICE : That's exactly it . . . Yes . . . He's right.

LAWYER *louder* : He is mistaken . . . because it is that very
fact that clears my client.

*Several close-ups of members of the crowd: a one-eyed
crook, a prostitute, an older man who looks like a
wrestler. They all look puzzled.*

THE ONE-EYED CROOK : Hey, just a moment, that's enough.

*We see other faces in the crowd. In the foreground a
crook with a moustache, a hat and a bow-tie.*

CROOK : Are you mad, you drunken old sot?

LAWYER : It is this very fact of obsession which makes my
client not responsible . . . And nobody can be punished for
something which he is not responsible for.

Whistles and cat-calls. Quick shot of a part of the crowd.

VOICE : That's ridiculous.

PROSTITUTE *furious, jumps to her feet* : Do you want to suggest by any chance that this *brute* should get off?

A CROOK *bitterly* : That he should stay alive?

Camera cuts back to the LAWYER *and the* MURDERER.

LAWYER : I mean that this man is sick. And a sick man should
be handed over, not to the executioner, but to the doctor.

105

Cut to the SAFE-BREAKER *in three-quarters profile, the angry crowd behind him.*

SAFE-BREAKER : Could you guarantee he'd be cured?

LAWYER *resume on him* : What use are asylums, then?

Medium shot of SCHRANKER, *the* CON-MAN *and the* PICK-POCKET, *seated at the table.*

CON-MAN : And what would happen if he escaped?

SCHRANKER : Yes . . . or if they released him as harmless? And what if the compulsion to kill returns? Yet another man-hunt for several months. Paragraph fifty-one again. Into the asylum again and then another escape or release. And then the compulsion all over again. And so on and so on till doomsday!

LAWYER, *shot of him* : No one has the right to kill a man who is not responsible for his actions. Not the state, and certainly not you. The state must take care that this man becomes harmless and ceases to be a danger to his fellow citizens.

During this plea, the crowd becomes excited and they begin to shout and bawl at the top of their voices. His last words are almost lost in the general laughter. Camera cuts in to a group of onlookers gathered below an enormous heating pipe. They are laughing. A PROSTI-TUTE *gets up.*

PROSTITUTE : You've never had children, eh? So you haven't lost any either. But if you want to know what it's like to lose one of your kids . . . *Another woman tries to calm her* . . . then go and ask the parents of those children he got at.

We see different groups of onlookers. In their midst an enormous thug listens close to tears.

PROSTITUTE *off* : Ask them what those days and nights were like when they didn't know for sure what was up . . . and about the ones when they finally knew what happened. *Camera cuts back to her, screaming* : Ask the mothers! *Cut to the* MURDERER *still crouched against the barrier, his hands over his ears.*

A WOMAN *off* : She's right!

Cut to a medium close-up of the MURDERER *who crouches ever lower, then cut back to the* PROSTITUTE *who repeats her cry.*

PROSTITUTE : Ask the mothers!

106

VOICES : Yes, the mothers . . . the mothers . . . ask them . . . Do you think they'll have mercy on a child-murderer?

Another group of onlookers is seen. The fever rises.

A CROOK : She's right.

ANOTHER : And how.

PROSTITUTE *off* : No mercy . . . No pardon . . .

A CROOK : Give him to us, the murderer.

2ND CROOK : Kill him, the beast.

We are shown several different faces in the crowd. A PROSTITUTE in the front row screams her rage. Behind her, a crook in a cap is also worked up.

YOUNG PROSTITUTE : Crush him, the brute.

MAN *at the same time* : Kill him.

Camera cuts to other faces already seen.

WRESTLER : Bleed the beast.

ONE-EYE : Hang him.

A VOICE : Beat him down.

A LITTLE MAN : Kill him.

ANOTHER : Kill him.

We see the whole furious mob.

CRIES : To the gallows . . . Finish him . . . Kill him . . . Kill him . . . Kill him.

Camera cuts quickly to the LAWYER.

LAWYER : All that shouting won't silence me.

The noise dies down. Another general shot of the crowd shows them waiting, but not appeased.

LAWYER : I will not allow a crime to be committed in my presence. I demand that this man . . .

A VOICE *interrupting* : He isn't one !

LAWYER *carrying on* : . . . that this man be granted the protection of the law, which is everybody's right.

A VOICE : To hell with that . . . hell with it.

Whistles and shouts from the crowd.

LAWYER *very loud* : I demand that this man be handed over to the police.

Cut to a high shot of the crowd and the leaders of the tribunal, in uproar.

A WOMAN *hysterically* : To the police !

CON-MAN *furious* : Filthy stooge !

The excitement is at its height. Everyone shouts, whistles and screams at the same time. From every side, crooks and prostitutes throw themselves towards the MURDERER *. . . then, suddenly, everyone freezes, and eyes fix on the door of the cellar.*

VOICES *and shrill whistles off* : Police . . . Hands up!

Taken by surprise the crooks and women all stand with raised hands. Only SCHRANKER *remains seated. He tips back his chair arrogantly. Having cast a long look round the assembled crowd and seen that there is no hope, he also gets up and raises his hands. (Still on page 112) The* MURDERER *still crouches against the barrier. He rises even more slowly and looks round in absolute terror. Camera comes in closer and a hand is placed firmly on his shoulder.*

A VOICE : In the name of the law ..

The music of Peer Gynt is heard. Fade to black.

After a short pause the voice of MRS. BECKMANN *can be heard* : We, too, should keep a closer watch on our children.

THE END

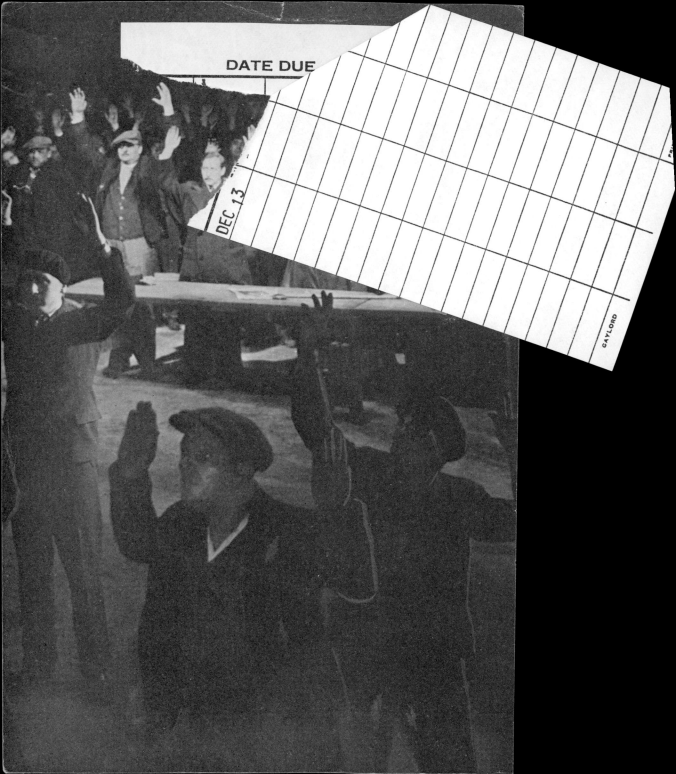